A Decolonial Philosophy of Indigenous Colombia

Global Critical Caribbean Thought

Series Editors

Lewis R. Gordon, Professor of Philosophy, UCONN-Storrs, and Honorary Professor, Rhodes University, South Africa

Jane Anna Gordon, Associate Professor of Political Science, UCONN-Storrs

Nelson Maldonado-Torres, Associate Professor of Latino and Caribbean Studies, Rutgers, School of Arts and Sciences

This series, published in partnership with the Caribbean Philosophical Association, turns the lens on the unfolding nature and potential future shape of the globe by taking concepts and ideas that while originating out of very specific contexts share features that lend them transnational utility. Works in the series engage with figures including Frantz Fanon, CLR James, Paulo Freire, Aime Cesaire, Edouard Glissant and Walter Rodney, and concepts such as coloniality, creolization, decoloniality, double consciousness and la facultdad.

Titles in the Series

Race, Rights and Rebels: Alternatives to Human Rights and Development from the Global South, Julia Suárez Krabbe
Decolonizing Democracy: Power in a Solid State, Ricardo Sanin-Restrepo
Geopolitics and Decolonization: Perspectives from the Global South, edited by Lewis R. Gordon and Fernanda Bragato
The Existence of the Mixed Race Damnés: Decolonialism, Class, Gender, Race, Daphne V. Taylor-Garcia
The Desiring Modes of Being Black: Literature and Critical Theory, Jean-Paul Rocchi
Decrypting Power, edited by Ricardo Sanín-Restrepo
Looking Through Philosophy in Black: Memoirs, Mabogo Percy More
Black Existentialism: Essays on the Transformative Thought of Lewis R. Gordon, edited by danielle davis
A Decolonial Philosophy of Indigenous Colombia: Time, Beauty, and Spirit in Kamëntšá Culture, Juan Alejandro Chindoy Chindoy

A Decolonial Philosophy of Indigenous Colombia

Time, Beauty, and Spirit in Kamëntšá Culture

Juan Alejandro Chindoy Chindoy

ROWMAN & LITTLEFIELD
Lanham • Boulder • New York • London

Published by Rowman & Littlefield
A wholly owned subsidiary of The Rowman & Littlefield Publishing Group, Inc.
4501 Forbes Boulevard, Suite 200, Lanham, Maryland 20706
www.rowman.com

6 Tinworth Street, London SE11 5AL, United Kingdom

Copyright © 2020 by Juan Alejandro Chindoy Chindoy

All rights reserved. No part of this book may be reproduced in any form or by any electronic or mechanical means, including information storage and retrieval systems, without written permission from the publisher, except by a reviewer who may quote passages in a review.

British Library Cataloguing in Publication Information Available

Library of Congress Cataloging-in-Publication Data

Names: Chindoy Chindoy, Juan Alejandro, 1983- author.
Title: A decolonial philosophy of indigenous Colombia : time, beauty, and spirit in Kamëntsá culture / Juan Alejandro Chindoy Chindoy.
Other titles: Time, beauty, and spirit in Kamëntsá culture
Description: Lanham, MD : Rowman & Littlefield, [2020] | Series: Global critical Caribbean thought | Includes bibliographical references and index.
Identifiers: LCCN 2020001706 (print) | LCCN 2020001707 (ebook) | ISBN 9781786616296 (cloth) | ISBN 9781538148303 (paper) | ISBN 9781786616302 (epub)
Subjects: LCSH: Camsa Indians--Philosophy. | Camsa Indians--Rites and ceremonies. | Indians of South America--Colombia--Sibundoy Valley.
Classification: LCC F2270.2.C25 C55 2020 (print) | LCC F2270.2.C25 (ebook) | DDC 980/.01--dc23
LC record available at https://lccn.loc.gov/2020001706
LC ebook record available at https://lccn.loc.gov/2020001707

Contents

Preface	vii
Introduction	xiii
Notes	xxiii
1 Time in Kamëntšá Culture	1
I. Time as History	3
II. Time as Primary Experience	17
III. Conclusion	35
Notes	37
2 Beauty in Kamëntšá Culture	45
I. Bëtšknaté as Constituted Symbol: Origins and Cultural Transformations	47
II. From Bëtšknaté to Clestrinÿë	51
III. Bëtšknaté as a Constituting Symbol: An Experience of Dancing	52
III. The Philosophical Significance of Kamëntšá Dancing	57
IV. Conclusion	59
Notes	59
3 Spirit in Kamëntšá Culture	63
I. Native Doctors and Rituals of Healing: The Constituted Nature of Rituals	64
II. Scholarly Descriptions of Yajé	66
III. Yajé Ceremonies in Sibundoy: The Constituting Aspects of Yajé	73
IV. Wind Symbolism and Metaphysics of Human Existence	80
V. Conclusion	82

Notes	84
Conclusion	89
Bibliography	93
Index	97

Preface

It was with some trepidation that I once embarked on writing the book that I present here. Part of the difficulty came from knowing that I did not have the luxury to remain neutral of the arguments that I am presenting. Part of it emerged from my life experiences. Living in two seemingly opposite worlds, one in which dreams, stories, and intuitions were true to life, while the other in which objective, public evidence counted as the source of truth, I used to feel that I could not adjust myself to either, not entirely. These worldviews emerged early in my life and took different meanings later. Before discussing more formally, it might be useful here to include a biography of myself, a confession, to indicate the personal motivation behind this project and the inevitability of including personal stories in it.

I was born in the rural areas of Sibundoy in 1983, when Colombian legislation still entrusted the Catholic Church with the "civilization" of the "savages." Both my parents and grandparents went through such legislation, which they have described it to me as socially diminishing and personally painful. Forced to learn Spanish in a school system ruled by discipline and punishment, they had to maintain their native language and their stories in private, only to be told with confidence under the protection of moonlight or uncommon sunny days in the Sibundoy Valley. A year after I went to elementary school, the Colombian Constitution, after a lengthy discussion, changed. This change resulted from social mobilizations of natives and peasants of the western mountain range of Colombia and students of public universities of the center of Colombia and political activism of various rebel groups in different parts of the country. One of the most significant of the changes came from Colombia's legal recognition, for the first time in its history, that it was a multi-ethnic and pluricultural country. In the 1991 Colombian Constitution, a fundamental principle, explicit in Article 7, states that the State recognizes and protects the ethnic and cultural diversity of the country. Although a bit late for much of the Colombian indigenous population whose sense of culture and language had been vilified, this recognition still became a symbol of hope for those who felt that the dawn of the day when one could speak one's language with pride and admiration had finally come.

Unaware that I carried a burden of a shameful past, I went through elementary school without a feeling of alienation. I almost naturally assumed that my parents spoke the Kamëntšá language because they did not have a chance to go to school and that they would talk to me more in Spanish than in Kamëntšá because they wanted me to succeed. As I do not remember having been discriminated against by teachers or classmates in elementary school because of my indigeneity, being spoken to in the Kamëntšá language at home and in Spanish at school was not an issue in my life. If it was, I did not experience it directly. Devout Catholics, my parents had me in the Champagnat School, led by the Marist Brothers who had come to Colombia at the beginning of the last century but who, along with other Catholic congregations, started to take part in the education system of Sibundoy after the Capuchin mission left in 1969. Because he could not study as he wished it, my father dedicated the best energies of his youthful years to giving all his six children the best education in town available at the time. He believed the Champagnat School had the best education in Sibundoy. Because of his dream, I never had toys with which to play at home, but always had all the best materials that the school required.

After my elementary school, I went to high school, and my experience was slightly different. Now a teenager, I became aware that there seemed to be a distinction between living in downtown Sibundoy and living in the rural area where I had always lived. My first troubling experience came when in a geography class, the homework was to provide the address number of my home in my neighborhood and to locate it on a map. Not only had I not been asked about my home place before, but never had I thought that it would be difficult to explain to other people that I did not live in a neighborhood but in the countryside, which had a native, not a Spanish, name and which did not have an address number. Never had I been confronted to explain to other people my location, which was dear to me but which might not make sense to others. Had I answered my teacher's question, "*Atšbe barië sensetbemá atšbebëtsetsangbe posadok, na machindinoy induabaynetš,*" meaning, "I live with my parents in Machindinoy," I would have been the subject of contempt and mockery, as I knew that the language I learned at home should not be used at school. My mom told me that I should be honest with my teacher and write in my homework that I could not answer the question because I did not live in the urban area and that the place where I was born is called *Machindinoy* in my native language. The thought that all my classmates had an answer for the homework different from mine, that everyone knew their neighborhoods well enough and that I did not have one, haunted me. My older sister helped me out with my homework that day. Thinking that the teacher did not intend to visit us, we made up an address number of the farthest part of Sibundoy and so I never wrote that I lived in Machindinoy. The answer for the homework went along well, but in my mind, a feeling of alienation started to grow. I later understood that there was a difference between living in Sibundoy downtown and living in the rural area.

My father used to take me to work on the farm during vacations from school. As a teenager, I learned to milk, inject, and take care of the cattle. I also learned to plow and harvest corn, beans, tomatoes, and a variety of fruits. When I returned to high school after each vacation, the meaning of living in a rural area started to be different from my elementary school years. My hands coarse, my skin darker, and without stories like my classmates, I became more and more alienated. While my classmates discussed their trips to different cities of Colombia, some of their expensive travel to beaches and others their travels to relatives who lived in other parts of Colombia, I had to find excuses not to talk about my experiences. I could not come up with a story that looked like theirs. Without too many friends, I almost failed the first two years of high school. My father was frustrated. He told me that if I did not want to study, I should start thinking that the life ahead of me would be like his, or even rougher. My mom gave me solace with her prayers. I ultimately managed to pass all my classes. But I had already started to dislike social sciences and to have found more comfort in formal areas of study. I soon became passionate about math, physics, and chemistry. My favorite class was algebra, as it offered me the illusion of creating secure systems of thought in which the solution to problems was precise, without signs of ambiguity or without involving anything personal.

As I loved those areas of study, I remember that I became enthusiastic on hearing of the composition of the universe. Lecturing on ancient atomic theories, Mr. Javier Erazo, my chemistry teacher, once said that human curiosity had led ancient cultures to investigate the ultimate components of reality. He indicated that in a serious study of chemistry, one might not only find the solutions to our health problems, but also the answers to questions of what makes us human, since, he said, from a theoretical point of view, we were made up of chemical structures like other living organisms. In related terms, Mr. Juan Carlos Escandón also spoke. As a mathematician and physicist, Mr. Escandón once suggested that the universe, as we see it with our eyes, is somehow illusory, that behind our natural attitude there lies a mathematical formula to be discovered. Since I had won a reputation of being a good math student when I was a junior in high school, I did not feel alienated for having been born in a rural area anymore. What before was a disadvantage, my condition of not having a TV or a radio, now meant for me that I had more freedom to think about the possibility of finding explanations not only of the final composition of our brain but also of the whole universe. I continued working on vacation with my father, but I was more and more enthusiastic about becoming a teacher. In my dreams, I wanted to be a math, physics, or chemistry teacher. I had my future sealed.

The same year when I thought I had already set up the dreams of my life, I was working with my father, like I used to do on vacations. But something changed all of a sudden. Weeding a cornfield on a sunny afternoon, I became extremely sick, almost out of nowhere. I had lunched well, but I felt drained, my energies waning. Concerned, my father advised me to make the effort of going to my grandfather's house, as he had already a reputation of being a good healer. I remember that I had been taken to his house a couple of times when I was a child but had never been there by myself as a teenager. When my grandfather saw me, he started to joke with me, as he usually did in his visits to our home. This day I did not have the spirit to follow his jokes. I managed to tell him that I was sick and that I needed him to help me. Soon he prepared himself to heal me, brought his medicine plants, and gave me some medication. Then he suggested to me that I rest because I was as pallid as paper ash. As I was resting, I had a terrible dream. I dreamt that strong black bulls were chasing me. Trying to escape, I jumped from a cliff into a deep well. As I was falling into the well, it became a whirlwind. As I fell, another deeper well would come in front of me. It felt like I was falling into an infinite abyss. When I woke up, I heard my grandfather speaking in Kaméntšá with my grandmother, asking her to give me some food as I woke up. Hungry as I was, on hearing this, I went directly to the kitchen. Asked by my grandfather how I felt, I said I felt renewed and thanked him. Curious, I inquired of him about my dreams, and he indicated that they are the signs that dangerous winds had whipped me. I wanted to inquire more about this, but my grandfather was always in a jovial mood, and he started to make jokes about himself, and soon I forgot that I was sick. I later had similar experiences, which forced me to think that my existence was rooted in different places. Science, at least in the way it was taught to me, had made me believe that precision and clarity, backed up with public evidence, was not only real but offered the most precious truths to human life. And at the same time, based on my sudden sickness, I knew that my nightmares and dreams were as real as the air I breathed. The medicine of my grandfather and his prayers were as true to my life as the fact that I could calculate with precision the solution to a problem in Baldor's algebra. And yet the experiences with my grandfather were telling me about the reality of a world in a more personal, more subjective form, in ways not experienceable by everyone.

From these personal experiences, I soon was moved to philosophy. I first tried to be a priest, thinking that it might help me understand the spiritual life of humans and the nature of the divine. I went to Bogotá to become a

Catholic priest, but after a year and a half, I quit. I did not feel myself sufficiently consistent, on the one hand giving people sermons of fidelity, hope, courage, and reliance on Jesus, but on the other hand thinking more that I wanted to have sexual experiences with young beautiful women. When I quit the seminary, my father, who had supported me economically, became extremely disappointed. As I could not help myself, I took a rather dark path in my life. I became an alcoholic and a compulsive smoker, and my life lost all its purpose. Without the help of my older sister and my grandfather, I could have probably ended my life. My older sister, who at the time was in Manizales, invited me to visit her and encouraged me to study. I did not have too many options; on the one hand, my test for admission to the university indicated that I should study anything related with natural sciences, but I had lost interest in them, as the result of my nightmares and the experiences I had and because I did not want to do anything related with farms. I was more interested in something like religion and mythology, but without belonging to a church. I wanted to keep reading what I had read in the seminary, but my high school records clearly indicated that I was not likely to get into the social sciences. I had to wait one semester and then I was admitted, I think in the last place, to the philosophy and literature program at Caldas University. The year was 2004. Since then I have dedicated myself to studying the significance for human life of cultural values, like my grandfather's, which I learned at home. But it took me a couple of years to finally figure out that the purpose of writing my dissertation in philosophy was more a personal commitment and less a professional enterprise, though I must admit that I could have not written this work without thinking that I have a professional responsibility to address the symbols of my culture, in a way in which the symbols transcend my idiosyncrasy. It became the project of my life in the summer of 2014.

I had started my PhD at Southern Illinois University in Carbondale in 2013. Because I had the fortune to be in a pluralistic program, I attended classes of different philosophical orientations with the hope that they would eventually guide me through the quest for meaning and for the kind of work that I knew I wanted to write but which I did not know how, and of which I was skeptical to discuss openly with my professors. More and more I became interested in the kind of philosophical approach that leaves the possibility of inquiry open. This open attitude became clear to me in the classes of American philosophy that I took in 2014 and 2015. In summer 2015, I decided to remain in Carbondale, motivated more by the openness and the pluralistic spirit of the philosophy department and the quietness of the town, and less by the pervasive conservatism of the town. I found consolation in books, in playing soccer, and to some extent in the writings that took a bit of risk, especially the works of Emerson, James, and Dewey. Despite my admiration for them, I did not want to write about them, nor dedicate my life to scholarship about them, at least not without addressing at the same time the concerns of my personal life. The words of Emerson, that the American scholar cannot afford to be a parrot of other people's thinking, had touched my mind and my imagination in ways that made me decide that I wanted to think and write about the symbols of my culture. Later, having read William James, I was more and more interested in reading more attentively the works of Native North Americans.

When I presented my prospectus in the fall of 2015, I still wanted the approval of my professors and decided that I should choose an American philosopher that had more impact on me. Thus, I indicated that I wanted to use William James's notion of radical empiricism to describe the experiences of continuity and discontinuity in the Kamëntšá culture. The feedback that I received reoriented my investigation, as my committee challenged me to be more specific about the kinds of experiences about which I was talking and the reason for my using William James's terminology. It was evident to me that I could still use William James, but that the primary purpose of the dissertation was to write about the Kamëntšá culture and its symbolic content, not William James.

The feedback was more challenging than what I had initially thought. Not only was I being confronted personally again, but the experience of not knowing how to explain to other people the values that were significant to me had haunted me again. I recalled my experiences of high school. This time it was not about making up an address for my home to get away from a geography class. This time the homework was to explain to people unfamiliar with my culture the values that have remained dear to me over the years. I was again planning to renounce philosophy altogether and maybe apply to a different program, like comparative literature. On reflection and after critical conversations with my friends from Colombia, some of whom were in the United States at the time, I realized that I was making an excuse, a rationalization of my fear to confront myself. My graduate committee had opened to me the possibility to do the research that I proposed, but I was making an excuse not to do it. After realizing that I had to confront myself, I experienced a kind of beautiful freedom that has guided me since then to read, think, and write about my own cultural experience and the significance of its symbols. It took some time to read and think carefully, and several hours of rewriting, to come up with the work of personal experiences and significant scholarship that I now present here. In writing this work, I can finally say that I have taken up a personal responsibility of confronting myself freely, without fear, at least without the fear of failing.

Introduction

The purpose of this book is to offer a philosophical account of the fundamental symbols of the Kamëntšá culture, an indigenous culture dwelling in the Colombian southwest. The main argument is that the experiences of Time, Beauty, and Spirit are crystalized in what might properly be called constituted and constituting symbols. Time in the Kamëntšá culture is crystalized in history and storytelling, Beauty in dancing, and Spirit in yajé ceremonies and other rituals of purification. I argue that this symbolic constitution of the Kamëntšá culture is a response to a quest for meaning. The notion of "constituting symbols" intends to account for the experiences of creativity, potentiality, and adjustment of the Kamëntšá culture to its historical and natural environment. It refers to the kind of meaning that emerges from imagining new possibilities of life, even in the face of hard social or natural challenges. The notion of "constituted symbols" indicates that the meaning and value of life come from a past, rooted in ritual, myth, and stories, all codified in the Kamëntšá language. The guiding question of this investigation is how to account for the quest for meaning coming from an indigenous culture. Using as example the culture that I know best, my primary hypothesis is that the answer to the quest for meaning lies in the most general living symbols of the culture in question, on those symbols that take hold of the past without losing its power in their antiquity, on those symbols that allow for new possibilities of imagining life. This introduction clarifies the fundamental concepts of this work, outlining the arguments exposed in the next sections and discussing the philosophical method used in this work.

"Sibundoy Valley" refers to the geographic space located in the southwest of Colombia, in the upper north of the Putumayo region, a place in which the Kamëntšá and the Inga culture coexist and share similar cultural patterns, despite their sharp linguistic differences. Properly speaking, Sibundoy is the heart of the Kamëntšá culture, and it is the point of reference for the history of the valley. At present, this valley is the home of four different towns, Santiago, Colón, Sibundoy, and San Francisco, and two corregimientos, San Andrés and San Pedro. Corregimientos are small jurisdictions relatively autonomous in their political organization but ultimately economically dependent on the towns; San Andrés is a corregimiento of the municipality of Santiago, and San Pedro is a corregimiento of Colón. The Inga population is present most notably in the towns of Santiago and Colón and the corregimientos of San Andrés and San Pedro. The Kamëntšá population mainly dwells in the village of Sibundoy but is also present in the town of San Francisco. The missionaries of the Capuchin Order created San Francisco and Colón at the turn of the twentieth century with the purpose of settling a white population. At present, the white population (and mestizos) dwells mainly in the downtowns of the valley while natives reside in the rural areas, with a few exceptions. Cultural hybridization has been more common between the two native groups and less frequent between whites and natives of either indigenous community.

In this book, when I discuss an issue that affects or a concern that is shared by both Inga and Kamëntšá groups, I simply write "natives of the Sibundoy Valley." When I discuss specifically the Kamëntšá group, I refer simply to the Sibundoy natives or the Kamëntšás. The reason for distinguishing the Valley of Sibundoy from the town of Sibundoy is historical. Sibundoy is the oldest of the villages in the valley. In 1700, Carlos Tamabioy, the legendary leader of the valley at the time, legally documented all the lands of the valley and used the approval of the Spanish crown to cede this territory to both Ingas and Kamëntšás so that no white people would later claim possession of them. With his deed, the west part of the lands of the valley become officially Inga territory. To be sure, the Ingas had lived with the Kamëntšás for a long time, recognizing their roots in the ancient Inca empire.

The arrival of white people at the turn of the last century as well as of the Capuchin mission to the Sibundoy Valley changed the political, economic, and social organization of the region drastically. White settlers and the Capuchin mission complemented each other. Arguing that the division of land was out of mutual consent with the natives, the Capuchins divided first the Kamëntšá and then the Inga territory. In 1903, they split the Kamëntšá territory into two: one for the natives, the historical town of Sibundoy, and the other for the whites, the village of San Francisco. Similarly, in 1911 they divided the Inga territory into two, one for the native Ingas, the town of Santiago, and another for whites, the city of Sucre, which later became known as Colón. The Capuchins created San Francisco with the argument that the division of the Sibundoy lands would bring peace and tranquility among "all" the inhabitants of the Valley of Sibundoy. They founded Colón with the argument that prosperity and civilization of Sibundoy would only be possible through the acceptance of the Spanish culture and the Catholic practices of the time. Practically speaking, with the foundation of those towns, the Capuchins helped legalize white people's land robbery.

With suffering and hope, with resiliency and fear, since the second decade of the last century, the Sibundoy Valley has gradually become a tapestry of native and white syncretism. Whether one crosses over this beautiful valley from east to west or vice versa, one can see that downtowns mostly remain centers of white people, while surrounding areas remain living enclaves of native culture.

If at present one takes the highway from Pasto, the capital of Nariño, to the lowlands of the western Amazon, one must cross over the Sibundoy Valley and see the four distinct towns, each within ten minutes' distance driving. Coming from Pasto, one first meets the city of Santiago, to which the corregimiento of San Andrés is attached. After ten minutes driving, one reaches the town of Colón, to which the corregimiento of San Pedro is affiliated. The San Pedro River is traditionally considered the mark that distinguishes the lands of the Kamëntšás from those of the Ingas.

The purpose of chapter 1 is to provide a view of how Time takes a symbolic meaning. The first part of the chapter discusses Time as history. A reason for accounting for this kind of historic time as experienced by the Kamëntšá culture is because current scholarship concerning the spiritual life of the Kamëntšá culture mentions its historical conditions briefly, without indicating how these historical circumstances have affected the process of symbol making. It should be noted that to describe time as history from a native perspective means to describe a specific process of colonization. But it should also be noted that this is only one experience of time. The most profound manifestation of time is not historical, but the time that flows in the experience of storytelling. The first chapter starts with an account of the experience of Time as history, which is to say, from a description of time as coming from a process of colonization that started in Sibundoy in 1535 and reached its highest form in the first decades of the twentieth century. Using scholarly documents and a few testimonies, I indicate that this process of transformation not only caused the natives of Sibundoy to lose their land but also brought about an image of the natives as the dregs of society.

As already mentioned, the purpose of describing the experience of time as history is to indicate that a study of the living symbols and rituals of the native communities must consider the historical and material conditions. Without so doing, one runs the risk of assuming that the spiritual life of the natives has remained frozen in time, unaffected by the material conditions. As I explain later, all scholarship concerning the native cultures of Sibundoy rests on two doubtful related premises: either the material conditions have not affected the spiritual life of the Sibundoy Valley, in which case one can talk about native spirituality without addressing the material conditions, or they have affected it so deeply that it is almost impossible to distinguish the native elements from those imposed by the missionaries. Such premises, typical of scholars who have visited Sibundoy, lack solid reflection. All symbols of the Kamëntšá culture reflect a historical awareness of the spiritual roots that come from the sacred place of origin along with creative responses to the imposed European elements, embodied here in the Spanish culture of Catalunya and the white peasantry of the Colombian population. Speaking from a Kamëntšá's view, one cannot speak of the symbols of a culture without knowing its place of origin and how this place takes meaning in Time.

After describing Time as history, I move onto the second part of chapter 1 to address the experience of time as storytelling. The main claim is that storytelling is the oldest constituting and constituted symbolic form of the Kamëntšá culture. The premise upon which this claim rests is in the idea that Kamëntšá stories emerged out of the feeling of relationality that the ancestors experienced temporarily in the Sibundoy Valley, which for them became the sacred place of origin, *bëngbe tabanok* in Kamëntšá language.[1] The place of origin takes deep meaning not because of the location, but out of the continuity of meaning created in Time. With intimate stories, the ancestors made the Sibundoy Valley a home. *Oy*, the locative suffix in Kamëntšá language, which indicates place of origin in words like *Sibundoy*, *Shonjayoy* (San Pedro creek), and *Vinyioy* (windy place) and which now remains in most of Kamëntšá's last names, such as *Juajibioy*, *Dejoy*, and *Mutumbajoy*, harbors the feeling of personal belonging to a sacred place.[2] These personal and collective experiences of relationality of the elders with their place of origin took value and acquired meaning in the form of stories. Stories not only immortalized the sacred place of origin of the ancestors but also provided continuity of meaning and orientation to the life of subsequent generations. It is, then, a manifestation of the experience of time; not of time as history, but a form of time more qualitative, more tuned with the sentiment of the continuity of experience. In the act of telling and retelling, and in the creative effort to transmit personally meaningful stories, the ancestors created a cultural narrative, its significance coming not only from the content of the story but from the act of telling it. It is sufficient here to invoke the patterns of land cultivation in Sibundoy as an instance of the unfolding of stories and how Time becomes a primordial symbol of the culture.

When they cultivated the land, the elders reminded themselves of oldest times, of times in which they could speak with the plants, have revealing dreams with them, and listen to the voices of the winds. As they created patterns of land cultivation, they described these experiences in stories. Not only did these patterns of land cultivation later reach completion in the experience of telling stories that provide meaning, but they also became the fundamental subject of the conversations of days of walking that ancestors used to take for trading purposes. Kamëntšá women later would remember that they maintained the memories of those travels, weaving *tšombiachë*, belts in Kamëntšá language. Like Penelope weaved the hope of Odysseus's arrival, Kamëntšá women weaved the hope of a new generation to which the stories they had heard became meaningful. *Tšombiachë* serve now as a cloth to cover the stomach of women and newborn babies, and it indicates that its initial purpose was to cover the origin of life with meaningful stories. These belts are still weaved patiently, expressing the constant warp and weft of Kamëntšá thinking. If Kamëntšá thinking remains alive, it is in great part because women have managed to keep it alive, then in secret, now in daily conversations. When a Kamëntšá women makes *tšombiachë*, the past, the present, and the future come as pulses to her imagination. This act of weaving condenses the art of storytelling in Kamëntšá, for in storytelling, it is the act of telling along with the content of a story that provides meaning. The content of the story, in as much as it is reproductive of a content, cannot alone provide meaning. The figures of the belts that Kamëntšá women elaborate, while beautiful to contemplate and admire, do not create the aura of significance if no story is shared.

In studying the stories of the Sibundoy Valley, some scholars have distinguished between stories that speak of the divine, which constitute mythology, and stories concerning human deeds, which belong to the field of folklore or legendary heroes. While this distinction might be useful to describe the difference of the content of stories, it is not useful to account for the experience of time that is revealed in the act of telling stories. On the other hand, if by "mythology" one understands that a story is meaningful in the sense of providing a purpose to life as it is related with the divine, and if by "folklore" one understands stories told with the mere purpose of keeping records of heroes, one can see such a distinction in Kamëntšá storytelling because there are clear instances in which the content of a story refers to divine forces while in other cases the story takes on human deeds. Despite this theoretical distinction, one should be careful to not commit oneself more to applying a theoretical category of interpretation than to describing what is at stake in the experience of storytelling. To be sure, the distinction between myth and folklore is foreign to Kamëntšá culture. If one applies it to stress one characteristic of the culture, one should be aware of not forcing too much a theoretical distinction into a living experience of time. Since the leading idea of the second part of chapter 1 is to provide a view of Time as experienced within the Kamëntšá culture, showing that storytelling gives an account of such a Time, it is worth remembering that the distinction between mythology and folklore ultimately falls short in accounting for the experience of storytelling in the Kamëntšá culture. Instead of using such a distinction, it is better to use a Kamëntšá expression, *botaman jenoiunayan*, meaning "let's have a beautiful and meaningful conversation,"[3] to indicate that the meaning of stories does not come merely from their content (to which the distinction between myth and folklore can be applicable) but also from the act of telling them (to which the distinction is useless).

In chapter 2, I turn to a study of *Bëtsknaté*, Kaméntšás' dancing ceremony, as it is celebrated today, and I claim that this dancing is the symbolic manifestation of the experience of Beauty. I demonstrate that dancing is the expression of the creative impulse of the Kaméntšás that emerged from cultural exchange and interiorization of experiences of other native groups of the region, most likely the result of Kaméntšás contact with other native groups of the lowlands of the western Amazon and the Andes. My central argument of this chapter is that Bëtsknaté is a celebration of the beauty of life as it comes, with suffering and hope, with fulfillment and frustration. It is not a representation or an expression of personal feelings or a mere religious sentiment; it is not a way of worshipping nature, but an aesthetic enactment of the fundamental forces of existence. It is a living celebration of life. I argue that since the dancing condenses the cumulative aesthetic experiences of artists, healers, and storytellers, it is at once a constituting and a constituted symbol of the culture. In its constituting element, it actualizes a sense of collective purpose and unity among the Kaméntšás, a sense of unity and purpose that requires dealing with suffering and failures, with the hope that we can forgive each other and do our best to celebrate our existence. It is, so to speak, a living expression of the desire for Beauty, which, in the Sibundoy Valley, is historically rooted in the place of origin.[4] It is through this annual dancing that Kaméntšás commemorate the experiences of suffering and prosperity, of resilience and endurance, of past and present.

Bëtsknaté is a dance of reconnection with *Tsbatsanamamá* (Mother Nature) and with other families (*Nÿetska Pamiliang*). It is a constituted symbol because part of its meaning comes from foundational stories and a foundational ritual of forgiveness. But the act of celebration, I argue, makes it a constituting symbol because in the dancing there exists an enactment of the beauty of life as it comes.

In chapter 3, I turn to a study of the Spirit, claiming that in the Kaméntšá culture Spirit is enacted in the ritual of yajé. The main claim is that the yajé ritual presupposes an ontology of the winds.[5] For the Kaméntšá culture, winds not only are physical realities that touch the human body, but also have a deeper meaning, a kind of metaphysical reality that affects the spiritual life. Harboring positive and negative energies, springing from old times and from actions of the present, winds manifest a spiritual common reality that precedes the existence of the individuals. Winds can be healing or harmful. They are metaphysical in the sense that they are understood as transcending the reality of an individual and of the culture itself. Because of this special ontology, one can understand that it is primarily through winds that one can sense the presence of a spiritual reality in the Kaméntšá culture. The members of this culture interpret other manifestations of human life, like dreams, as ultimately signs of winds deeply stored in human life. When they are not perceived immediately, winds are interpreted as energies that remain in the body and become dreams, nightmares, or electric pulses in the human body. Nothing has haunted more the imagination of Kamëntšás than dreams. One of the earliest books that was published in Kamëntšá language by Kamëntšá speakers was on the interpretation of dreams.[6] As I explain in chapter 3, the meaning of dreams comes from a careful interpretation of spiritual reality in the context of the ontology of the winds.

The ontology of winds is fundamental for comprehending the ritual of yajé. As it is practiced in the Kamëntšá culture of today, the yajé ritual comes from a careful enactment of the ontology of the winds. Kamëntšá native doctors who lead rituals of yajé ought to develop intimate relationships with the winds in ways that other people, including harmful doctors, cannot. They describe their activities as the result of personal experiences in which they are called by winds to become doctors. Very often these are bountiful winds that reveal themselves to those who are capable of spiritual fortitude, enduring suffering, and humility. Without proselytizing themselves, most doctors see themselves as servants of the powers of nature and guides to the spiritual dimension of human existence. Familiar as they become with the manifestations of the winds, native doctors can free a person from his or her bad winds and give back his or her good winds. The knowledge of plants by native doctors comes from their capacity to sense and conspicuously concentrate on the forms of winds that plants store.[7] In as much as the effectiveness of healing in rituals of yajé depends on the ontology of winds, it should be considered a constituted symbol of Kamëntšá culture. Scholarship concerning yajé ceremonies adequately indicate that yajé comes from the lowlands of the Amazon. According to Melvin Lee, there is empirical evidence indicating that Kamëntšá elders had knowledge of the properties of a species of *Danturas*.[8] In as much as the yajé ritual came from the contact of Kamëntšás with other native groups of the lowlands of the Amazon, it has a history and is thus a constituted symbol of the culture. However, the ritual of yajé is also a constituting symbol, in the sense that it provides meaning and orientation to the individuals who participate in it and, by extension, to the whole community. The transformative effects of individuals participating in yajé rituals intend to carry a well-being to the community too.

The Spirit of the Kamëntšá culture can certainly be imagined differently, without necessarily arguing that the loss of ancient practices of healing would immediately imply the vanishing of a culture. But it is useless for the moment to ignore the potency that those rituals have had and continue to have in the Kamëntšá culture.

Finally, to conclude the ideas here presented, I briefly discuss the political challenges of maintaining Sibundoy as a sacred place of origin of the

Kamëntšá culture in this century in the Colombian context. I take on the experiences of Time, Beauty, and the Spirit, as they are manifested in the Kamëntšá culture. After showing how the Kamëntšá culture has created its symbols to address the quest for meaning from a specific place in the world, I argue that the quest for meaning, while experienced differently in different cultures, is also common in the most general terms. I take as a hypothesis that human cultures have a desire to organize their most fundamental concerns in terms of experiences of Time, Beauty, and the Spirit. I take as a working hypothesis that these aspirations are common among human beings.

Taking into account the experiences of people might contribute to a more careful conversation on the menacing forces that affects indigenous cultures in general, especially the unyielding idea that native peoples are behind progress and civilization. We all know that the expression of this idea comes very often in the way governments intend to create highways or exploit the land without the consent of the peoples who have dwelled in places before governments themselves were created. The purpose of these political comments is dual. First, I intend to point out a political problem common in the Americas. Second, I intend to show that more informed political conversations on the lives of natives requires an understanding of how they have responded to the human quest for meaning.

The study here presented is about the constituted and constituting symbols of the Kamëntšá culture that address the question of meaning in human life in the most general sense, in the sense that tries to answer to the question of how Time, Beauty, and Spirit are experienced in a native culture. While in most of the chapters I describe the material conditions that menaced and continue to menace the quest of meaning within the Kamëntšá culture, the main purpose of the work is not about the material conditions for the quest of meaning. Its main purpose is to demonstrate that the experiences of Time are both as history and as storytelling, that Beauty is best manifested in the dance of forgiveness, and that the Spirit is experienced in ceremonies and other rituals of purification.

My study of the Kamëntšá symbols takes a comprehensive approach from life experience. The main criticism that I elaborate against previous scholarship on Kamëntšá culture is its fragmentary approach. As I will demonstrate in this study, descriptive scholarship of Sibundoy fails to explicate the meaning to human life that emerges from the symbolic constitution of a culture. As an introductory remark here, let it suffice for the moment that I merely cite three representative cases of well-documented scholarship of the Sibundoy Valley that ultimately fail to address the quest for meaning.

In a well-documented investigation on Sibundoy ethnobotany, Melvin Lee Bristol in 1965 classified the plants that Kamëntšás hold dear, sacred, and useful, some of which were unknown outside of the valley.[9] While studying ethnobotanics with Richard Evan Shuttles at Harvard University,

Bristol set forward to investigate the properties of a plant that according to Shuttles was unique to Sibundoy. In 1965 Bristol came to Sibundoy with his wife and stayed there for two years, exposing himself to the Kamëntšás culture and the Catholic priests of the time. He observed, wrote, and classified the plants that he deemed crucial to his investigation. Sensitive to the cultural milieu that underlies the criteria of utility, adornment, and healing to the plants of Sibundoy, Bristol paid special attention to the plants that Kamëntšás hold most dear, the *Danturas*. Nonetheless, Bristol's writings failed to explicate the spiritual relationship that Kamëntšá people have established with the plants of the valley and the stories that the ancestors elaborate with those plants, neglecting thereby to account for the meaning of plants to the inhabitants of this place. In a similar manner, Haydée Seijas's 1969 PhD dissertation, "The Medical System of the Sibundoy Indians of Colombia," addressed the practices of healing and the rituals of cleaning, without explaining the ontology of the winds invoked by native doctors in their practices.[10] Seijas follows the writings of Bronislaw Malinowski and describes the rituals and the cultural practices of the Kamëntšás. While she distinguishes diseases caused "naturally" and "mystically," she does not explain that the rituals of healing presuppose a way of understanding the world in terms of its spiritual dimension, which takes its roots in the notion that wind is ontologically different from other beings.

Finally, in *The Sayings of the Ancestors*, John McDowell offers a detailed account of the stories of the elders and tries to decode the spirituality of the natives of Sibundoy by studying the sayings and the interpretations of dreams.[11] While his approach is sound, McDowell ultimately is committed to applying the theories of previous anthropologists and folklorists, unfamiliar with the experiences of Sibundoy, more than to describing the life experience of time of the natives of the Sibundoy Valley. McDowell declared that the Sibundoy spirituality must be understood in more general categories of interpretation, like myth, folktale and *oicotype*.[12] He suggested that this allows us to comprehend the nature of folk religion. Neglected in McDowell's works is that Kamëntšás see their stories and their experience of Time dynamically, not statically.

The philosophical method employed in this work is radically empirical, in the sense suggested by William James. James started to work on his notion of radical empiricism as early as 1884 when he published "On Some Omissions of Introspective Psychology."[13] In this seminal essay, James criticized the classical British empiricists who reduced experience to a series of distinct elements and did not account for the dynamic, continuous quality of consciousness. "Our mental life," wrote James, "like a bird's life, seems to be made of an alternation of flights and perchings." James articulated later his position of radical empiricism in his 1909 book, *The Meaning of Truth*, where he defined radical empiricism as a postulate, as a statement of fact, and as a generalized conclusion. As a postulate, radical empiricism demands philosophers to debate about things definable in terms drawn from experience. As a statement of fact, radical empiricism affirms the reality of conjunctive and disjunctive relations between things; and as a generalized conclusion, it asserts that the parts of experience hold together from next to next by relations that are themselves part of experience.[14]

While James did not apply his notion of radical empiricism to the study of cultures, I use his assertion and his method, showing that conjunctive and disjunctive relations are part of an experience and as real as the things that they relate.[15] I take this to be a sound methodological approach to a philosophical investigation on the symbols of native cultures. Core symbols of indigenous cultures cannot be mere representations or abstractions from experience; they must account for the specific natural and historical environments and must reflect vitality. In describing the Kamëntšá symbols as constituting and constituted, I am considering their historical determination, their continued vitality, and their potency. My explicit recognition of this methodology should not be confused with the general purpose of the study here presented. To be sure, I do not intend to present this work as a cultural embodiment of the thought of William James. If the arguments and the conclusions of the present work allow such an interpretation, it should be taken as a secondary point, for the main purpose of the present work is to provide a philosophical interpretation of the symbols of the Kamëntšá culture of the Sibundoy Valley in Colombia. In combining descriptive scholarship of the Kamëntšá culture with stories I have heard in Sibundoy, I offer a more comprehensive and more empirically grounded approach into the nature and meaning of cultural symbols that address the quest for meaning from a specific culture. The study here presented also takes some personal experiences that intend to illustrate the main points, hoping that they do not distract from the main argument.

The word "symbol" in this work is not merely used as a substitution for an elusive object. The way I am using it is in the sense of a living force, a grounding element that constrains the answers to the quest for meaning. Storytelling, for example, is a symbol of life in time as experienced by the Kamëntšá culture. As a symbol, it accounts for the act of telling a story and for the meaning of what this act creates among the people who are listening. When one listens to a story, one participates, not in a frozen idea in time, but in a process that informs the present and inspires the future.

Another key term that I use in this work is "experience." This concept echoes the philosophical works of William James and John Dewey, who both understood it as the result of activities of living organisms within their environments, from which meaning emerges. While James emphasized the more intimate, the more subjective kinds of relationships of human experiences, Dewey was more interested in accounting for the kinds of experiences that result from the interaction of the organism with its environment and take on general traits. Because Kamëntšás' understanding of the world is of immediate relatedness with the rest of the environment, of feelings, memories, and creations of meaning, one can speak of Kamëntšás' experience more in terms of James and Dewey than in other forms of empiricism like those of traditional British empiricism like Locke or Hobbes.

My appropriation of the term "radical empiricism" should be understood as the best methodological tool that I have come across in Western philosophical tradition to explain adequately the living meaning of my culture to philosophers interested in learning about other rich cultural determinations of life, not to those whose primary interest lies in constantly applying a traditional philosophical concept to all aspects of existence. In addition to disputing British empiricism, William James also used "radical empiricism" to indicate that the determinations of existence vary among different peoples. While he did not develop his pluralism, he was aware of the different ways that humans find significance in life. Using "radical empiricism" as a tool to facilitate comprehension of the cultural determinations of Kamëntšá life should therefore not lead any readers to conclude that the main purpose of my work is to typify or validate James's thinking at the expense of the Kamëntšá culture. Nor should it lead anyone to suggest that no philosophical interpretation would have been drawn from Kamëntšá culture without James's thinking.

I want to stress that the sense in which I use the terms "constituted and constituting symbols" is meant to account for the historically formed symbols, rooted and culturally appropriated in the Sibundoy Valley; as constituted, symbols are forces of the past that provide meaning to the present. By indicating that symbols are also constituting, I intend to point out that they are not understood by the community as symbols frozen in time. On the contrary, they are understood dynamically, alive, spurring creativity and innovation, with potency, leaving room for novelty. In those symbols hinge Kamëntšás' memory and its continuity, the possibility of brotherhood and its actual fulfillment, and the continuity of imagining the world relationality.

NOTES

1. *Sibundoy* is the word used since 1535. Elders say their ancestors called it *Tabanok*, to the place. All Kamëntšá words or expressions introduced in this work will be freely translated. While some efforts to systematize and have a "standard" description of the Kamëntšá language have been made, there is not yet a consensus on how one should properly write in Kamëntšá. I provided the translations within the text, or in parentheses. For example, in some cases, scholars write "Camëntsá" instead of "Kamëntšá." I follow the more common usage, "Kamëntšá."

2. At present Sibundoy has distinctive Spanish denominations of its neighborhoods. Not long ago, it used to have different native names: Tabanok was in the center of the Sibundoy Valley; the northeast was *Juachenoy*; the northwest, *Setesoy*; the north, *Octacjbiaio y*; the

southwest, *Wabjajanayoy*; the southeast, *Fšajayoy*; the south, *Chĕnguanoy*; and the southwest, *Bushajoy*. The suffix *oy* remained in all those denominations.

3. The word *botaman* means "beautiful" in the moral and ethical sense.

4. As I will make clear in chapter 2, the Ingas who live mainly in Santiago, San Andrés, Colón, and San Pedro dance the *Atún Puncha*.

5. To a certain extent, this ontology of the winds can also be found in the cultural expressions of the Inga peoples.

6. Justo Jacanamijoy España, Juan Bautista Jacanamijoy Juajibioy and Carlos Jamioy Narváez, *Camĕntša Cabĕngbe Ntšayanana* (Sibundoy: Uámana Soyĕnga Camĕntšañe Uatsjéndayĕnga, 1994).

7. Some elders attribute their knowledge of plants to visionary experiences in yajé ceremonies.

8. In 1965, Melvin Lee Bristol, during his stay in Sibundoy to complete his Harvard dissertation on Sibundoy ethnobotany, wrote that several kinds of Dantura are known exclusively from the Valley of Sibundoy. Describing the use of Danturas in Sibundoy, Bristol describes seven types of Danturas but centers attention on the use and cultivation of *mutskuai borrachera*, the culebra type of Dantura. Cfr. Melvin Lee Bristol, "Sibundoy Ethnobotany" (PhD dissertation, Harvard University, 1965), 269–85. Bristol follows closely Richard Evan Schutles's writings, who in 1955 described *culebra borrachera* as a plant that the Sibundoy use in divination, prophecy, therapy, and witchcraft. Schutles had visited Sibundoy in 1942 and 1946. Cfr. Richard Evan Schutles, "A New Narcotic Genus from the Amazon Slope of the Colombian Andes," *Botanical Museum Leaflets, Harvard University* 17, no. 1 (1955): 1–11.

9. Bristol's study offers a detail taxonomy of the plants of Sibundoy, in Kamĕntšá, Inga, Spanish, and English, but his interest lies more in describing plants and less on explaining the relationship between plants and the habitants of Sibundoy. Cfr. Melvin Lee Bristol, "Sibundoy Ethnobotany" (PhD diss., Harvard University, 1965).

10. Haydeé Seijas, "The Medical System of the Sibundoy Indians of Colombia" (PhD dissertation, Tulane University, 1969).

11. John Holmes McDowell, *Sayings of the Ancestors: The Spiritual Life of the Sibundoy Indians* (Lexington: University Press of Kentucky, 1989). While in this book McDowell takes on the Inga peoples of the town of Santiago and the corregimiento of San Andrés, he believes the sayings that he documents belong to the Sibundoy spirituality. After his documentation of the Inga peoples, McDowell takes on a more detailed exploration of the stories of the Kamĕntšás, suggesting that the stories come from an initial burst of spirituality at the beginning of the times. McDowell published his interpretation of Kamĕntšá storytelling in *So Wise Were Our Elders*. His main argument is that in Kamĕntšá narrative there is a distinction between mythology and folklore. Cfr. John H. McDowell, *So Wise Were Our Elders* (Lexington: University Press of Kentucky, 1994).

12. McDowell concludes *Sayings* arguing that "the Sibundoy case must be viewed as an instance of what folklorists call an *oicotype*, a regional manifestation of the general scheme, and it may well contain details that will help flesh out the existing documentary record." With this claim McDowell is basically recusing himself from accepting that the natives of the Sibundoy Valley have developed their own ways of understanding the world. Even if some of the traditions at present performed in Sibundoy came from the interactions with other native groups of the region, the cultural embodiments of those traditions should not merely be regarded as different clothes of the same scheme.

13. William James, "On Some Omissions of Introspective Psychology," *Mind* 9, no. 33 (January 1884): 1–26.

14. William James, *Writings 1902–1910* (New York: The Library of America, 1987), 826–27.

15. William James, *Essays in Radical Empiricism* (Cambridge, MA: Harvard University Press, 1976), 23–24.

Chapter One

Time in Kamëntšá Culture

The experience of time in the Kamëntšá culture is crystalized in history and storytelling. The first part of this chapter tackles Time as history, with the purpose of providing a context of the material conditions in which the Kamëntšá's symbolic responses to the quest for meaning have emerged. The second part of the chapter addresses Time as storytelling. In the two sections of this chapter, I indicate that the lands of Sibundoy, from the Kamëntšá's view, are not only a material element to possess but the grounding of the symbolic meaning. Land is both symbolic (*Tsbatsanamamá*) and material (*fšants*).[1] This conception of land comes from synthesizing temporal experiences. Space, the physical environment, is a conception grounded in temporal experiences. The most tangible manifestation of space is obviously the material (i.e., land as *fšants*); but this conception of physical space presupposes *Tsbatsanamamá*. In other words, the conception of space as material comes from a process of having understood the experience of time.

Although this chapter initiates with a description of Time as history, this should not imply that the experience of Time in the Kamëntšá culture has only been in the form of history. On the contrary, the main idea is that Time as history reflects only one form of time, its immediacy. The experience of time as storytelling is more significant for the Kamëntšá culture, and it takes its form before, during, and after the arrival of the Spanish conquistadors.

In addressing the documents from the times of the Spanish conquest and the subsequent arrival of missionaries to the valley, I hope to demonstrate that the experiences of Time in the Kamëntšá culture did not start with the Spanish Conquest nor were they obliterated by it. Despite the humiliating conditions in which they were forced to live at the turn of the last century, the natives of Sibundoy managed to keep alive part of their stories, keeping them alive in the land from which those stories emerged.

In the first part of this chapter, I provide a documented overview of the experience of Time as history, accounting for the origins of the Sibundoy Valley from the elders' view as reflected in their conversations. I start with an account of the origins of Sibundoy from the Kamëntšá perspective, and then I cite historical and ethnolinguistic scholarship to indicate that land cultivation patterns and Kamëntšá familiarity with the plants that grow in the valley suggest that a civilization in progress had been taking shape before the arrival of the Spaniards to the area in 1535. Then I discuss the process by which the Sibundoy Valley became part of the feudal system of encomienda with the arrival of the Spaniards and the way in which the Kamëntšá language changed significantly.[2] Of those early colonial times, I also describe the story of the Lord of Sibundoy, which reflects how the natives of Sibundoy embraced gradually Catholicism without the constant presence of missionaries. After discussing the arrival of the Spanish, I present briefly a history of land ownership as inherited by the great Cacique Carlos Tamabioy in the year 1700. I conclude this historical overview with an extended discussion of the Capuchin mission and the arrival of white settlers at the turn of the last century. I present evidence to suggest that the hardest form of colonization in Sibundoy dates to the last century.

In the second part of the chapter, I discuss Time as storytelling. The memory of the ancestors of Kamëntšás, stored at present in the art of storytelling, refers to the lands of Sibundoy as the origins of life and culture. When asked of the origins of his or her being, any Kamëntšá elder answers, "*Bëng [agem] Kamëntšá intšang, Kamëntšá biyang,*" ("We and our thinking emerged here)" in plural, because in the sentiment of a native elder it is crystalized in the idea that a personal question of one's origins involves the origins of the culture itself. The idea of location, on which the immediate affirmation of the origins depends, takes us to an experience of time that is manifested in the sacredness of a place and in the aura of significance that it provides for its inhabitants. The word "Kamëntšá," which results from combining an adverb of place, "muentš," meaning "here," and the affix "ka" meaning "how," accentuates twice the experience of intimacy with the place of origin. The term "Kamëntšá" is a condensed version of a longer expression, "Kamëntšá intšang, Kamëntšá biyang," meaning, "We are from here, and we speak the language that emerged from here."[3] There is no other language like ours, the Kamëntšá elders used to insist (linguistic investigations now confirm the view that Kamëntšá is an isolated language). A Kamëntšá sense of existence is deeply linked with and to some extent defined by the language of this place.[4]

At present, the Kamëntšás and the Ingas alike, despite the historical displacement from their own land, still describe the Sibundoy Valley personally as a home. For the Kamëntšás, the valley is *Tsbatsanamamá*, an honorable-sacred mother; for the Ingas, *Pachamama*. As a home, this place binds human creatures from birth to death with an unyielding symbolism, with special potencies that manifest themselves in dreams and winds, making it possible for new generations to find and recreate meanings of life until the arrival of the time to rest would come. I am still part of the generation that enacted the ritual of tying oneself with the place of origin. I have heard that not long ago, when a child was born, half of its umbilical cord was buried under the home's kitchen fire, linking the life of the individual to the grounding force of the land. Thus attached, part of the significance to human life comes from knowing one's origins. Elders believed that this ritual would also give them peace at the end of their life, as part of their bodily existence will be reconnected with that part buried at birth. The valley is thus a symbolic milieu wherein a sense of origin and existence is so profound that it makes no sense to describe it in terms of a detached object.

Scholarly descriptions of the Sibundoy Valley refuse to include personal accounts to this place, in part because they have been written by nonnative scholars. Even those who find evidence to say that the history of the Sibundoy Valley does not start with the arrival of the Spaniards find it difficult to assert the historical feelings of intimacy and the continuity of time of this place. Based on ruins of ancient agricultural terraces in some parts of Sibundoy, Lee Bristol, for example, indicates that the Sibundoy Valley had been the home of at least one thousand habitants in "prehistoric times." To judge from his writings, prehistoric times refers to the times before the arrival of the Spanish conquest. While Lee Bristol indicates that it is not possible to judge with certainty when those terraces were constructed,[5] he indicates that archaeological evidence suggests the presence of indigenous peoples "at an earlier epoch, or the influence of a cultural expansion from the Peruvian region (where terraces are still cultivated extensively), or the remains of a now extinct culture."[6] Bristol is right to indicate that the agricultural terraces that he saw indicate agricultural developments prior to the arrival of the Spaniards to the valley, as all stories, including the most sophisticated ones that are woven by women in their sashes, make reference in one or another way to memories of land cultivation. The memory of Kamëntsá ancestors also indicates that Sibundoy has always been the sacred place of origin of life and culture. The Kamëntsá language, after years of comparative linguistic studies, yet remains an isolate language, further proving that the origins of Kamëntsá culture rests in the Sibundoy lands.

I. TIME AS HISTORY

At present, all scholars of the Sibundoy Valley agree that its native inhabitants *met* the Spanish conquistadors for the first time in 1535. In the history of the Spanish conquest of Sibundoy, it is convenient to distinguish three periods. The first period starts in 1535, the time of the first *meeting*, and ends in 1700 when native leader Carlos Tamabioy bought the lands of Sibundoy and filed a legal testament of the lands of Sibundoy so that all the descendants of Kamëntšás and Ingas lived there peacefully.[7] The second part takes up from the testimony of Carlos Tamabioy until the arrival of the Capuchin mission in 1893; the final segment takes from the Capuchin mission until 1991 when the Colombian constitution changed. While I do not want to offer a detailed account of each of the periods, I want to outline the material conditions that affect the temporal continuity of the symbols of the Kamëntšás.

All natives of Sibundoy remember that in 1535 the ancestors met Juan de Ampudia y Pedro de Añasco, captains of Spanish conquistador Sebastián de Belalcázar, who extended the conquest of Quito all the way up to the southwest of Colombia.[8] Citing the works of Ampudia and Añasco, a group of native scholars of Sibundoy keeps for their record that the first meeting by Ampudia and Añasco was in June 1535.[9] Other references indicate that it was in July of the same year. In the memory of the Sibundoyes and other historians, it is recorded that seven years later Ampudia and Añasco stepped in Sibundoy, in 1542, and Hernán Pérez de Quesada, obsessed with the search for *El Dorado*, crossed over the Sibundoy Valley, met the natives of Sibundoy, and conquered them.[10] Anthropologist Michael Taussig relates the journey of Pérez de Quesada's conquest and his 260 companions from Mocoa to Pasto. Coming from Mocoa, De Quesada and his men, says Taussig, lay close by "in the mountains rising to the west in a fabled land called Achibichi, where the Spaniards found the tillers of the Sibundoy Valley but not gold, and beyond that the new Spanish town of Pasto."[11] With the arrival of these early colonizers, the Sibundoy Valley became part of the Spanish crown, and all natives were forced to pay tribute. As it is well known to us, during the Spanish conquest, the lands of natives hosted feuds sustained by the encomienda system. An enslaving institution, the encomienda system provided Christian indoctrination in exchange for forced labor. Despite that, in 1520, Carlos V, and then his son Philip II, had technically *liberated* natives from forced labor, the Spanish provinces continued to tax the natives. The lands of Sibundoy, with the cold weather and the difficulty of access to it from any of the other colonized cities, remained relatively isolated. To be sure, except for the missionaries, there is no historical record of the white population taking over the lands of Sibundoy before the twentieth century. The effects of the encomienda system in Sibundoy, however, should not be underestimated. The *Archivo General de Indias de Sevilla* says that on November 25, 1570, there were 1,371 "tributary Indians" in Sibundoy,[12] suggesting that Spaniards frequently traveled to Sibundoy to collect tributes but did not remain there.[13] As they were forced to pay tributes to the Spaniards, the natives started to see that the sacred place of origin also became an object of exploitation and forceful labor.[14] The Kamëntšá expression *pamilie tributarie person*, which at present conveys the feeling of respect for another person, takes root in those early times of the conquest in which it was a duty to pay tribute to another person. As some official reports of the time indicate, the Sibundoy Valley became part of the encomienda system.[15]

i. Sibundoy at the Times of the Early Spanish Conquistadors

The first missionaries who came to Sibundoy were of the Franciscan Order; they stayed in the town from 1547 to 1577.[16] After they left, the Friars of the Dominican Order took over the task of converting natives of Sibundoy to Christianity, remained officially in Sibundoy until 1579,[17] and then they became occasional visitors. To judge from the stories of Kamëntšás, the linguistic changes of the native language, and the elements of religious syncretism, one can infer that it took early missionaries several generations to convince Kamëntšás of Catholicism.

A famous story in the Sibundoy Valley, which has different versions and which I heard for the first time in a public meeting, narrates the times when the early missionaries removed an icon of Christ from Sibundoy, causing some disagreement among the locals. Known today as the story of the Lord of Sibundoy, this story describes the process through which a form of native Catholicism took shape in Sibundoy. While the version that I present here provides details that are not present in other versions, the three main points of the story remain the same: it first tells that the Lord of Sibundoy came in a disguised form, as a native who did not know how to speak the language. Second, it explains how the icon changed location, and third, that he left, causing dismay among Kamëntšás. Here is the version I heard for the first time in a public meeting.

> The elders used to say that long time ago, on a sunny day a Kamëntšá man was piling up dry leaves at his *jajañ* [garden]. It would have been a typical day had he not noticed someone approaching him at a considerable distance.[18] The newcomer looked handsome, like another native, bare foot, and with a *cusma* [a traditional clothing worn by men] hanging from his shoulders.[19] But as he approached closer, it became evident that it was a white man wearing native clothes and speaking a rough language. Having been offered *bëkoy* (maize beer), he declined, impeding any possible communication. Confused, the Kamëntšá man went to report this incident to his family, some of whom believed him but others, not.[20]
>
> Days after the previous incident, the unknown man showed up again, now standing in front of all the brothers who were working together. Looking like a Kamëntšá from the outside, this newcomer did not speak in Kamëntšá and remained in no disposition of drinking *bëkoy*. He spoke in a rough language again. At first uncertain, the Kamëntšá brothers decided that they should consult with other neighbors in the village. In conversation, the Kamëntšá decided

that a house should be built at a distance from the heart of the village so that this unknown man could spend some time there.[21] They also agreed that the strange man should be given food and drinks.

But the unknown man did not stay at the house built for him. Instead, he decided to come back to the heart of the village. Every day he sat and spoke incomprehensibly, at the core of the Kamĕntšás' village. Such a defiant attitude proved to be offensive to many Kamĕntšás. After long conversations, the Kamĕntšás finally agreed to take the man by force, tied him to the house, and waited on the road to see if someone else was helping him. At dawn they saw that the man was on his way back to the heart of the village. On seeing this, the guards whipped him severely, and shortly after, the man left, causing dismay among many others. Such was not a way of treating the stranger, who also looked like a native.[22] The cross at the center of the plaza stands today in memory of that man, as the place where he wanted to be.[23]

As the story indicates, Christianity seemed to have entered the minds of the natives of Sibundoy in the early times of colonization. Historian Juan Friede,[24] following historian Rafael Sañudo, indicates that the first part of the story dates to the times when Dominicans left Sibundoy officially in 1579, taking with them a creolized image of Christ and causing thereby uneasiness among the natives.[25] To judge from the documentation of the ecclesial history of the Catholic Church in the Putumayo area which has overseen the Sibundoy Valley, the Dominican presence in Sibundoy lasted until the beginning of the nineteenth century. Haydée Seijas writes that even in the second half of the eighteenth century, when there was no resident priest in Sibundoy, "missionaries from Pasto and later from Mocoa visited the Sibundoy Valley periodically."[26] The story of the Lord of Sibundoy should thus be taken as a story of syncretic religious continuity that comes from the early times of colonization until the beginning of the last century. It should not be taken as referring to a single episode.

ii. Carlos Tamabioy's Legacy in Land Ownership

While today he is well-known in the history of the indigenous legislation, the legacy of Carlos Tamabioy has remained virtually unknown to the public, except for a few missionaries of the Capuchin Order who wrote about the history of the missions.[27] It was only with the publication of Bonilla's book *Servants of God, Master of Indians* in 1969 that Tamabioy's legacy became fundamental to the defense of lands of Sibundoy from new forms of colonialism. Tamabioy's deed has become inspiring to Kamĕntšás' political leadership. No other native of Sibundoy has yet surpassed his legacy. The figure of Carlos Tamabioy remains sacred among Kamĕntšás and Ingas in the sense that his legacy refuses to become part of the annals of folklore. All natives of Sibundoy interpret the deeds of Carlos Tamabioy as sacred, as the true protector of their lands. In the minds of natives, the memory of Tamabioy intensifies the symbolic meaning of land itself. Any suggestion that Tamabioy is a *legend* created by the Natives of Sibundoy to claim land ownership is false and suggests that there is no *real* evidence to say that Ingas and Kamëntšás own the lands of Sibundoy.

Carlos Tamabioy was born in the second half of the seventeenth century. Tamabioy's leadership resulted from his self-training on the legislation and the formalities of the time. He spoke in Spanish like a wholehearted Catholic. One can read from his testimony that before explaining his will concerning the lands of Sibundoy, he invokes God as a Catholic, saying, "In the name of the Father, the Son, and the Holy Spirit, Amen,"[28] invoking then the saints of the Catholic Church and Virgin Mary. Subsequently, and as witnessed by Spaniards Commissar Ignacio Pérez de Suñiga and Don Gaspar de Leon, he proceeds to indicate that he wishes the lands of Sibundoy to be enjoyed by the natives, those residing in Santiago and those dwelling in Sibundoy. Having provided the boundaries of the lands of the valley, which at the time consisted of 12,000 hectares,[29] he then concludes his wish for a Catholic sepulture when he dies. Finally, he asserts the signatures of the witnesses, dating the deed of March 15, 1700. A copy of this testament has remained with the natives of Sibundoy since then. In 1952 Capuchin Priest P. Jacinto Ma de Quito was writing the history of the town of San Francisco in the Sibundoy Valley and claimed to have seen a copy of the testament of Tamabioy in the hands of Francisco Tisoy. De Quito indicated that lands of Sibundoy cost Carlos Tamabioy 400 patacones, a currency of colonial times, which were paid to the King of Spain.[30] Despite the documented will of Tamabioy, the borderlands of Sibundoy have remained subject to slow exploitation of a few whites, the most devastating of which dates to the beginning of the last century.

Seventy years after the testament of Tamabioy, the natives had already lost about two square kilometers of land in the north of the valley. The Ortiz family had slowly started to take the lands of the Sibundoy to pasture cattle. Using the expressed will of Carlos Tamabioy, Leandro Agreda, then the ruling leader, traveled to Popayan, walking several days to reach the office of the governor of Popayan, a city 311 kilometers from Sibundoy. As he saw the governor, Agreda complained that the natives of Sibundoy could not continue to pay taxes because the Ortiz family had started to take more and more land.[31] With the idea that he was asking for justice regarding the ancestral territory so that the natives could pay the taxes, Agreda convinced the governor of Popayan to dispel the Ortiz family from the Sibundoy territory. But the Ortiz family had already managed to "negotiate their property," to another landowner, don Simon de la Barrera. De la Barrera, claiming that he had paid the Ortiz family, finally managed to settle down "this dispute" and took possession of about two square kilometers in the north of the Valley of Sibundoy, namely, the lands of Abuelapamba and Juachinchoy.[32] After this loss of territory, and because of the burgeoning independent movements across Latin America, the natives of Sibundoy retained relative control of their lands, except for a volcanic explosion in Pasto, which in 1834 caused inundation and earthquakes in the valley, forcing some families to move to different places within the valley.

iii. Capuchin Missionaries and the Division of Land in the Sibundoy Valley

The relative tranquility that Sibundoy natives had over the lands in the first three-quarters of the nineteenth century started to dwindle away gradually with the arrival of white populations and the Capuchin mission to Sibundoy at the turn of the twentieth century. The missionaries of the Capuchin Order came to Sibundoy in 1893 and remained until 1969. Law 35, passed on February 27, 1888, allowed Colombian presidents to negotiate with the Vatican the presence of Catholic missions in different regions of Colombia without the approval of Congress.[33] Using this legal tool, former president Rafael Reyes arranged with the Capuchins from the province of Catalunya the taking over of the mission of the southwest of the Colombian Amazon, with the headquarters in Sibundoy. Both the Capuchins and the Colombian government agreed that Colombian natives ought to be "civilized." The 1888 law also gave political and juridical power to missionaries. Using this legal support, the Capuchins believed that their presence was not only politically justified but morally needed. Claiming that the prosperity and well-being of the natives depended ultimately on endorsing Catholicism, the cattle industry, and the Spanish language, they started to create infrastructure projects that would implement those ideals. They regulated the creation of new towns, churches, schools, and land ownership in the Sibundoy Valley.

At their arrival in Sibundoy, the Capuchins saw that while the natives had already embraced the spirit of Catholicism wholeheartedly, the material progress that they envisioned had not yet arrived. As they equated material progress with Spanish progress, the Capuchins, as far as historical records at present indicate, did not object to the presence of white settlers in Sibundoy. On the contrary, they believed that a white presence in Sibundoy was justified, in part because they believed that the white population would contribute to the progress of the town, as white settlers brought in the cattle industry and spoke Spanish. In part taking advantage of the privilege that the Colombian government had given them, and in part actively lobbying in the cities of Pasto and Bogotá, the Capuchins set forward a "civilizing" project that at present we know favored the white settlers more than the natives. Claiming themselves to be the bastion of human reasoning and the highest model of human life, the Capuchins exerted civic and police power in Sibundoy, dividing the lands of the natives as their logic dictated.

Criticism of the Capuchin mission in Colombia started from the very beginning of their arrival. Pasto's liberal newspaper *Eco Liberal* was begun to give voice to some native leaders who denounced the excessive work that missionaries forced on them. Because of their influential political power, Fray Montclar, the leader of the Capuchin mission, convinced his conservative political friends in power that the newspaper had become politically active against the Church and the conservatism of the time, claiming that the criticisms came from political opponents who wanted to attack the Church and its friends, downplaying the native's complaints.[34]

In 1968 Colombian sociologists Victor Daniel Bonilla published a well-documented scholarly book, called *Siervos de Dios, Amos de Indios*.[35] Bonilla's main argument is that the Capuchin mission in Sibundoy used the political and legal power not only to conquer natives spiritually but also materially. Using the writings of the Capuchins, photographic evidence of the time, and written testimonies of natives archived in provincial and local government records, Bonilla concludes that from the arrival of the Capuchins, the natives of Sibundoy lost about half of their territories. Current scholarship, along with some testimonies of my grandparents, confirm Bonilla's thesis.

Using as a main source the writings of a Capuchin historian, Fray Jacinto Ma de Quito, who lived in Sibundoy and wrote a history of the foundation of a new town, we can now confirm Bonilla's general thesis. Contemporary historians, including Capuchin historians, now admit that the actions of Capuchin missionaries, especially their support of white settlers, changed the living conditions of the Kamëntšá culture dramatically. Take as an example of this drastic change the history of the foundation of the town of San Francisco, written by a Capuchin Fray, Jacinto Ma de Quito.

De Quito writes that the history of the foundation of the town of San Francisco in the lands of Sibundoy started with an idea of Capuchin priest Lorenzo de Pupiales, at birth known as Apolinar Chavez Portilla. De Pupiales had come to the town of Sibundoy in 1900 with the purpose of educating the children of the region. On his teaching and living experiences, Fray Lorenzo de Pupiales noticed how shocking it was to see antagonisms between white and native children. White settlers had come to the valley along with the missionaries, many enticed by the idea of taking part in "vacant lands" in Sibundoy. While living in the Sibundoy Valley, De Pupiales came to know that the main reason for the antagonism between white and native children reflected a deeper antagonism; whites had taken lands from the Sibundoy natives. As he mentioned it explicitly, the antagonism between whites and natives came from "the fact that the whites had taken unjustly and even on bad faith the lands of the natives. The natives, seeing themselves in detriment in their own lands, seedings, and homes, started to distance themselves from the center of the town and to take revenge upon their oppressors whenever possible."[36] Arguing that the best pacific solution must entail native concession of part of their ancestral lands to the new whites, De Pupiales and other priests managed to convince some native leaders that they must give away a portion of the lands that Cacique Tamabioy had left to them so that everyone could live in peace. Such was De Pupiales's motivation to build the foundation of a new town for whites. Clarifying the sentiment and motivation behind De Pupiales's idea of a new town for whites, historian Fray De Quito asserts that white people had come to Sibundoy because they were motivated by the possibility of exploiting quinoa and rubber in the region. This reason seems to lack historical foundation, as the Sibundoy Valley at the time remained isolated from the rest of the region, its main road coming to development through the insistence of Fray Fidel de Montclar in 1912. The geography and the climate conditions of the Sibundoy Valley impeded it becoming a land of rubber exploitation. [37] De Quito, however, insists that De Pupiales's motivation to create a new town for white people was to bring peace and tranquility to the region and to deter white people from taking further possession of native lands.[38]

Praising the work of Fray de Pupiales, De Quito also cites a part of his writings to show how the idea of a town for white people started. De Pupiales had written, "As I familiarized myself with how the two races lived in the town [of Sibundoy], it occurred to me that there should be a foundation for the whites elsewhere."[39] Such an idea in the mind of a Capuchin took practical effect in 1902, and it finally concluded with the Colombian Congress's approval. Law 41, passed on November 19, 1904,[40] supported the creation of towns like these and provided regulations to favor white settlers. De Quito asserts that while the idea started in the mind of De Pupiales, it became actual with the *consent* of natives themselves. With the help of other Capuchin predecessors, De Pupiales ultimately convinced the natives of Sibundoy that they should permit the division of the lands, arguing reasons of peace and tranquility. Commemorating the half-century of the foundation of the town of San Francisco, in 1952, Fray De Quito wrote and praised the labor of his co-religionary De Pupiales, emphasizing that natives convinced themselves of the Capuchin solution to give away part of the land to white settlers. De Quito writes, "For this time [when Lorenzo De Pupiales was in Sibundoy] there were three Caciques who *came to listen to reason* and worked with the priests so that other natives *consent* to give away the mentioned lands. These were Miguel Guajivoy, Mariano Guajivoy and Alejo Jamioy."[41] Evidence of this consensual agreement, according to De Quito, is a letter written by Mariano Guajibioy to the Bishop of Pasto, which dates to February 4, 1903. Indicating that he reproduces part of Guajibioy's letter faithfully, De Quito cites Guajibioy saying, "We [natives of Sibundoy] gave away the lands of Guaira-Sacha o San Francisco voluntarily for the poor whites to build there."[42] Despite this concession of land, the whites of Sibundoy were not satisfied. In April of 1903, the regional attorney of Pasto came to Sibundoy and decreed that the whites should be moved into the lands of San Francisco, which had been "generously donated" by the natives with the intervention of the missionaries.[43] Since its foundation, San Francisco not only has become a land for white settlers but a symbol of justification of legal appropriation of the lands of Sibundoy to favor white population. With the already mentioned Law 41 of November 19, 1904, the Colombian government gave explicit acknowledgment that the lands of Sibundoy belonged to the Kaměntšás and Ingas, as the testament of Carlos Tamabioy stipulated.

Implicit in this idea of consensual agreement to give up some land to benefit poor whites is that the Capuchin missionaries also knew that the lands of Sibundoy belonged to Kaměntšás and Ingas. This acknowledgment is historically critical, as later the Capuchins missionaries had to push for legal changes to further claim land ownership in different regions of the valley. When Fray Fidel de Montclar was the head of the Capuchin mission in Sibundoy, as current scholarship indicates, he believed that some of the lands of Sibundoy were "vacant," changing thereby the Church's attitude of protecting natives from whites to becoming the rulers of native lives.

In January 1905, only two months after Law 41, the Vatican appointed Fray Fidel de Montclar, who at the time was thirty-eight, Apostolic Prefect of Putumayo and Caquetá. De Montclar become the central leader behind the foundation of another town for white people, the town known at present as Colón, perhaps to assert upon natives with a European name the power of colonialism even in the most remote areas of Colombia. The creation of this town was a part of a more ambitious project of Montclar's leadership, the creation of a road of approximately forty miles that would connect the lands of Sibundoy with the Pasto province. The argument for this road was that it would bring progress and civilization to the Sibundoy Valley. In ten chapters (out of seventeen that compose the book), Bonilla offers a thorough explanation, citing official documents of Colombian legislation and of regional governmental archives, to demonstrate how De Montclar exerted powerful political decision-making that ultimately harmed the living conditions of the natives of Sibundoy. More recently, a new investigation by history professor Simón Uribe, from Antioquia University in Colombia, shows that De Montclar believed that the progress of the natives of Sibundoy depended on endorsing a white peasantry mode of life, taking as a model the Spanish culture.[44]

Discussing De Montclar's deed, historian Simón Uribe indicates that the road symbolizes the imposition of the civilizing order of the state over the native communities of Sibundoy. He says, "The history of the road can, at least in part, be read from this purely coercive dimension, and more explicitly as a creative destructive process through which the state violently attempted to conquer and expand into 'savage' territories and populations."[45] The construction of this road, as Bonilla and Uribe indicate, used cheap, forced labor of the natives of Sibundoy. In 1908, three years after being appointed Apostolic Perfect, De Montclar issued a code of regulations to govern the Indians of his jurisdiction (*Reglamento para el Gobierno de Indígenas*). Among the policies that he set up in this code, De Montclar made sure that it was up to the Church to settle any disputes of the lands of Sibundoy. With such policies, he literally stole the ownership of the land. As Bonilla suggests, he had become a servant of God and a master of natives. Included in Montclar's regulations was that natives could elect their leaders but only from those previously appointed by himself. As one can read in De Montclar's code for ruling the natives of Sibundoy, a native leader, once elected, becomes responsible for reporting the number of natives who would work in the construction of roads and public buildings. Also, elected native leaders would regulate the number and the cost of the "cargeros" (natives who would carry white traders or travelers on their back).[46] Uribe indicates that De Montclar's resolution also contemplated various crimes, such as "thievery, drunkenness, public meetings and parties, and the penalties established included compulsory work from 1 to 20 days."[47] Uribe also comments that while as early as 1909 missionaries in Colombia were forbidden to impose labor obligations on the native population, the Capuchins continued to force Sibundoy natives to work. To support this claim, he brings up a memorandum that indigenous authorities of Sibundoy presented in 1909 to the Pasto governor in which they complained that each of them was compelled to supply the mission with "100 or more workers per week."[48]

Bonilla and Uribe both indicate that De Montclar's political leadership and his lobbying at Pasto and Bogotá, insisting that the natives under his jurisdiction ought to be civilized and be given progress, influenced directly the creation of two pieces of legislation to the detriment of native land ownership. First, Law 51, 1911, disregarded the testament of Carlos Tamabioy in that it ordered the creation of a new town in the Sibundoy Valley, the town of Sucre, at present known as Colón. Second, Law 106 of 1913 and Law 69 of 1914 prescribed the *Junta de baldíos* chaired by the Governor of Nariño, the Apostolic Prefect (namely De Montclar), and five members of the Pasto City Council.[49] The practical consequence of these laws was that, under the leadership of Fray De Montclar, the lands of the Sibundoy Valley, which had been previously recognized legally as belonging to the Kamëntsás and Ingas, became lands at the disposal of the Capuchin leadership.

In 1970, two years after Bonilla's publication, Capuchin priest Ramón Vidal wrote an apology for the missions[50] in the format of a pamphlet. According to Vidal, Bonilla's study skewed the labor of the Capuchins and was written with the purpose of defaming the work of the missions. Vidal claimed that Bonilla used picturesque legends to elaborate malicious historical arguments and to ignore the educative leadership of Sibundoy to the advancement of civilization[51] and the consolidation of Colombia as a nation.⁵² Convinced that De Montclar and the Capuchins acted legally and according to the norms of the time, Vidal did not think that Bonilla's scholarship provided the Catholic Church reasons to ask forgiveness from the natives of Sibundoy, but instead he defended all missionary acts. Perhaps Vidal's most glaring justification came when he wrote that that native *cargeros* chose their *job* freely and that it was painful for missionaries and travelers to be carried sitting on the back of natives on the way from Pasto to Sibundoy or vice versa. Of the *cargeros*, he wrote, "It was a noncoercive service, organized by the natives, and of remuneration." And of the practice as such, he indicated, "It was the only possible means to access [those regions of Colombia], unlike urban areas." And, without any sense of shame, he concluded, "All white people who entered in these lands—including general Rafael Reyes, who later become President, had to endure such a servile act: for it was an authentic sacrifice to travel like that."⁵³ Vidal's preposterous account makes me imagine that my ancestors had a good time spending their wealth, at least to judge from the rising white population and missionaries who came into Sibundoy, all enduring such a painful way of being transported on the backs of natives. One is left with a certain stinging feeling when one thinks that the defense of the missions comes from a Capuchin member who in 1968 asserted that, to defend the actions of his co-religionary missionaries, one should think of the suffering of being carried on the back of a native. Vidal, however, was never alone in making these kinds of comments.

Chancellor and Priest of the Universidad del Rosario in 1912, Rafael Maria Carrasquilla, before a conference on the missions on October 20, 1912, praised the work of the Capuchins in Putumayo as exemplary for the nation. Central to Carrasquilla's argument is that light, progress, and civility arrived in the lands of the Sibundoy Valley thanks to the Capuchin missionaries. In his words, with the arrival and the work of the Capuchins, the hell-like lands of Sibundoy reached paradisiacal completion. Offering the view of a traveler who goes from Pasto to Sibundoy, Carasquilla writes,

> Going from the capital of Nariño to the missionary settlement in Putumayo, a traveler used to take a whole week, carried on the back of an Indian who with his hands and his feet would climb along the scary cliffs, on the edge of dizzy abysses, and who would then descend through hell-like precipices, like those described by Dante in the descent to Inferno. At present, it takes one forty-eight hours to traverse that distance, on horse-riding, over such a solid and almost even road, without danger and weariness.⁵⁴

Because he is writing in 1912, Carrasquilla is underscoring the progress of the Capuchin missionaries, and especially the leadership of De Montclar, for De Montclar was the most outspoken for the construction of the road from Pasto to Sibundoy. Contrasting the beauty of the Sibundoy Valley before the eyes of any of his contemporary travelers with the ugliness of the valley before the Capuchin settlement, Carrasquilla continues,

> Now the traveler gets into the Valley of Sibundoy, fertile and promising like the longing of a terrestrial paradise. Five years ago, it used to be a region of savages and beasts. Standing out today are five promising little towns with a church each; operating are therein several schools in which German women teachers have organized competitions on grammar and arithmetic, national geography and history, competitions worthy of any major urban city.[55]

And to conclude, Carrasquilla exhorts the audience to cooperate with the missions, as he believed that in them rested the future of the nation. To cooperate with the missions, he said to the audience, is to work in favor of "universal civilization, of the progress of the human lineage, as it is a sacred duty that patriotism commands us to fulfill, for it is necessary to make citizens out of today's savages."[56]

The arrival of the Capuchins to the Sibundoy Valley brought about two harmful effects to the Kamëntšá and Inga groups: exploitation of native land and collective disdain for native imaginary. With respect to land exploitation, Bristol and Seijas, while visiting the Kamëntšás in 1962 and 1964 respectively, reported that the majority of the Kamëntšá families had been pushed to the periphery, as the core of Sibundoy was mostly in the hands of the Church and white settlers.[57]

In the 1970s, the creation of the Colombian Institute for Agricultural Reform (Incora) and the Bureau of Indigenous Issues (Dirección de Asuntos Indígenas) lessened the power of the Church in native communities. Yet, two generations of Kamëntšás had already faced the forces of colonization with the arrival of the Capuchin missionaries from Spain and their apparent preference for making better the lives of white settlers, forcing natives in schools to believe that property and progress depended on embracing the lifestyle of the white population. The educational system brought in to Sibundoy by the Capuchins, the Marist Brothers, and the Franciscan nuns contributed to making natives feel ashamed of their origins and making them believe that the highest aspiration of a native should be to look, act, and speak like a Spaniard. In the generations of my grandparents and my parents, white settlers used racial slurs to offend natives. As the Church had judicial and political power until 1991, its members contributed significantly to such actions. When they created towns and displaced natives to the wetlands of Sibundoy and gave the most beautiful lands of Sibundoy to white settlers, the Capuchins reversed the Latin-American Catholicism, which, since the writings of Las Casas, had been in preference and defense of aboriginal Americans. Instead of preferring the humblest, the Capuchins followed wholeheartedly Colombian Law 89 of 1890, which until 1991 ordained Catholic congregations to educate with the purpose of erasing the elements of "barbarism" in indigenous peoples and making all Colombians full, mature citizens with adequate moral principles, following the model of the defeated Spain.

When I was a freshman, I was about to quit high school. I think my dad saw my discomfort, and as he could not afford my dropping high school, he started to motivate me to be like my older sisters, who both had become good students. As I told him that I had plans to become a farmworker like him, he told me part of his childhood experience. We sat down and drank chicha, and as I remember it, he started the conversation in this way:

> I did not study not because I did not want to but because I couldn't. I had to walk two hours every day to get to elementary school. I used to wake up at 4 a.m., eat something and start to walk through muddy roads, clean myself after in a river, and show up at school at 7 a.m. We used to meet with other native kids on our way, and we saw that white kids who lived in town sometimes walked with their parents. We did not talk too much with other native kids because missionaries would look at us suspiciously, since it was forbidden to speak in Kamëntšá. Everything was normal to me until I was in the middle of my fourth grade, and one night it rained heavily, so heavily that I could not even walk through the roads. For four months, Sibundoy bifurcated into two halves, only those in the north continuing the classes. The rest of us, all natives, had to quit school. As our parents knew from their own experiences, missionaries used severe penalties for native kids who did not show up to classes or did not do a good job. They also punished white kids now and then, but missionaries were more lenient to them. As for native kids, penalties ranged from remaining at the basement of the school without food for two days or kneeling on sharp little stones for one day without food. Sometimes professors would whip you with a ruler if you forgot what you wrote and erased yesterday on your small blackboard. Because of those painful personal experiences, families of the south decided ultimately not to send the kids back to school. It is because of this that I only learned how to read, do basic math, and write. Otherwise, maybe my life could have been different. When I became a young adult, strong that I had become through farm working, I studied a bit more. But first I had to dress like a white person to be admitted to working on farms in Pasto and Mocoa. Since then I abandoned our traditional garment, learned of bank regulations, cattle management, and laws of private property. We are now living in a different time: you have this wonderful opportunity to study; I can buy you notebooks, books, and uniforms. You don't have to go to a school where white kids would humiliate you because of your clothes or your language. Professors won't punish you physically. Hence, I do not see any reason why you cannot make yourself a bit of an effort and study. I wished I had the opportunity you now have.

As my father's story confirms, under the leadership of the missionaries, native children endured more penalties than white children, and the school system ban on speaking in Kamëntšá contributed to equating native culture with stupidity and lack of refinement. In helping to create such self-deprecatory images among the Kamëntšás, the Capuchins, as Bonilla quite accurately indicated, became servants of God and masters of Indians. The amount of land that the Capuchins took and the economic and political power that they exerted, which benefited white settlers and impeded natives, have led me to conclude that the arrival of the Capuchins to Sibundoy marked the most critical form of colonization under which my ancestors lived. Apologists of the missions have indicated that the Capuchins contributed significantly to the consolidation of native Catholicism and the Spanish language. As far as the Sibundoy Valley is concerned, Kamëntšás had already been devout Catholics when the Capuchins arrived. The document of Carlos Tamabioy, signed in Spanish by a wholeheartedly Catholic Kamëntšá two centuries before the arrival of the Capuchins, indicates that my ancestors had culturally embodied both Spanish and Catholicism.

The arrival of the Spanish conquistadors to the Sibundoy Valley splintered Kamëntšás' sense of continuity. The eyes of the ancestors had not yet seen individuals with such unwavering desires for land possession, not that they did have or know a concept that indicates material possession. It is not that they did not have any reflective story of destructive forces. They had stories of witches and bad winds that might come to visit and cause harm in response to a calling. But with the wave of white people coming to the valley at the turn of the century and their taking possession of the land, the ancestors realized that newcomers had a different understanding of the world, one dominated by material possession. The once wild creatures whose manifestation was in the realm of imagination at the turn of the century had become actual and more fearful than once imagined.

Before the twentieth century, the natives of Sibundoy, based on the contact they had with whites in previous centuries, might have conceived whites to be those people who wore helmets, squashing their thick and curly hair, and held dry mosses on their chins. And they likely imaged that the eyes of the colonizers were as gloomy as their skin. But at the turn of the century, this was not part of imagination anymore. It was a fundamental part of daily life that natives had to face.

With the arrival of the Spaniards, the once sacred place of origin, the home of the Kamëntšás, gradually became a place of struggle for land property, human dignity, and cultural survival. Protected by Andean mountains and its taxing climate, Kamëntšá elders enjoyed a relative isolation in the aftermath of the Spanish Conquest. While it became part of the encomienda system with the arrival of the Spanish conquistadors in 1535, Sibundoy remained in the hands of the Kamëntšá and Inga elders until the twentieth century. As the testament of Carlos Tamabioy indicates, at the beginning of the eighteenth century, the natives of the Sibundoy Valley had already embraced Catholicism and the Spanish language.

The Capuchin missionaries had arrived in Sibundoy at the end of the nineteenth century. Initially led by Colombian-born priests, the Capuchins followed the footsteps of missionaries who had tried to convert natives by persuasion and example. The foundation of the town of San Francisco, while orchestrated by the Capuchins on the basis of peace and tranquility, still recognized the testament of Carlos Tamabioy of 1700, which indicated that the Sibundoy Valley belonged to the Ingas and Kaměntšás. At the turn of the century, with the arrival of the Capuchins from Catalan, the mission took a different path. Under the leadership of Fray Fidel de Montclar, the Capuchin missionaries cast shadows of Catholic teachings, as they acted now contrary to the progressive side of the Church, which after the writings of Las Casas had believed that persuasion and living examples should convert natives.

The survival of the living symbols of the native cultures of the valley depended partly on the resilient character of its members, which led them to create bonds of friendship with other natives of the region, using Spanish as the main tool for communication. But this survival also depended on the spiritual fortitude of some of the elders. When they were forced to send their children to school, native parents encouraged their children to learn Spanish while never renouncing the indigenous languages at home or refusing to heal children with their rituals. The spiritual fortitude of some of the elders proved to be the most effective and culturally challenging method to the Spaniards. In conversation with Catholic priests, my grandfather noticed that Catholic priests could not find opposition between the experience of native spirituality and that of mystical theology in the Church.

The history of the Sibundoy Valley that I described in this chapter aimed to provide a sociohistorical context for discussing the Kaměntšás' and Ingas' symbolic responses to the quest for meaning. It is in the material conditions that I exposed in this chapter that one should find the answers for the gradual loss of cultural symbolism in recent decades and the need to reflect more carefully upon what the native cultures have learned, have lost, and have incorporated into their lives. Without knowing this cultural context, one's reflections on one or another symbol of the indigenous communities of the valley, however theoretically sound they might be, are ultimately disengaged from life experience.

II. TIME AS PRIMARY EXPERIENCE

Long before the need for its writing and affirming its origins and its telos formally, the Kaměntšá culture had recorded its most significant life experiences in stories, proverb-like sayings, interpretations of dreams, and songs. Stories about the animals, the sun, the moon, the corn, the water, the land, and the house had been shared from one generation to the next, always with the purpose of filling human existence with meaning. Humorous and more serious native stories of the Sibundoy Valley have put the power of speech into a sacredly dynamic form. The voices and deeds of the ancestors are invoked with intensity in healing and formal ceremonies. Stories orient the meaning of life.

Social self-determination as a distinctive group, in the sense of political affirmation looking after one's origins, took a narrative form later among the Kamëntšás. It happened when Kamëntšás traveled to trade with other native groups and when they learned of their differences in speech, food, and knowledge of plants, and it became a prominent form of expression when a string of Europeans came to conquer and destroy the lands of Sibundoy materially and spiritually. The practice of storytelling is at present alive, and it has become a symbol of the Kamëntšá and Inga cultures. A careful reflection on the ongoing meaning and practice of storytelling suggests that the Sibundoy natives are not living in a mythical past or in an utter state of colonial dependence. The tradition of storytelling has been dynamic and continuous in time, always reorienting human life within a dialogical framework with the purpose of seeking after meaning.

Scholarship concerning native oral traditions in the Americas associates storytelling with myth and ritual, suggesting that the narrative mode of being native consists in having a set of founding beliefs that go unquestioned in a society or a group, impervious to modification or reinterpretation.[58] Most of the scholarship concerning native storytelling takes for granted a distinction between mythology and folklore, the former relating the actions of the divine and the latter narrating human deeds. Such a distinction rests in part on ethnographic evidence that illustrates the existence of sacred stories that go unquestioned within a group and serve as the foundation of the customs and traditions of the culture in question. But the distinction also rests on the idea that the meaning of a story comes from its content, namely, of the fact that myths relate divine actions while folklore addresses human activity.

The experience of storytelling as practiced and reflected by living native scholars takes a different approach. Central to living indigenous cultures in the Americas is that the antiquity and content are not sufficient conditions for the sacredness of a story.[59] The act of telling a story, its purpose, and the responsibility of the speaker in the act of telling also contribute to the sacredness of a story. Using as an example the practice of storytelling in the Sibundoy Valley, I demonstrate that the main purpose of storytelling as practiced at present is that it functions as an enactment of continuous events that create meaning, not as a blind repetition of former deeds. The Kamëntšá expression, *botaman jenoiuyanan*, meaning, "let's dialogue meaningfully," indicates that the primary function of a story is that of creating meaning in time. Along with other forms of speech present in Sibundoy, the idea of meaning construction, *bëtaman jenoiuyanan*, illustrates the transformative power of storytelling, taking the past as a reference, as an *example* of how to create meaning.

In the three sections that follow, I want to show that Kamëntšá storytelling is a constituted and a constituting symbol in the quest for meaning. The core argument of the remaining text of this chapter is that the act of telling a story is fundamental, intrinsic to the meaning of a story. I initiate with a brief discussion of two different narrative modes of speech that are characteristic of the Kamëntšá culture regarding the constituted symbols in the creation of meaning: the ceremonial, or *bëtaman jalensensian*, and ritual, or *jashnayam*. After this, I present and discuss John Holmes McDowell's account of Kamëntšá storytelling in terms of constituted meanings. Following the distinction between mythology and folklore implicitly, according to which the former relates divine deeds that become foundational to human history while the latter narrates human heroism, McDowell provides an interpretation of indigenous storytelling of the Sibundoy Valley in terms of mythology. McDowell's interpretation needs substantial revision. The sharing of a story, the act of storytelling demands an analysis of meaning as constituted in time.

In all forms of Kamëntšá speech, the speaker takes on the language and the deeds of the ancestors. Common to ceremonial and ritualistic speeches is the speakers' attitude toward language as a unifying cosmic force: the speaker of ceremonial language links the present with the past and affirms the temporal primacy of the universe, the sky, the earth, and the community of former leaders. In so doing, the speaker creates an environment in which the past takes over the present.

A slightly different attitude takes place in familiar and dialogical narratives. First, in familiar and dialogical narratives, the speaker tells a story. But the act of telling a story emerges from the need to *reflect* on a mounting concern of the present, not merely for entertainment. Even humorous stories follow this logic: like all stories, humorous stories intend to respond to present concerns. The difference between ritualistic and dialogical narratives thus lies in that in the former the past outweighs the present while in the latter the present takes over the past. In familiar and dialogical narratives, the speeches and deeds of the elders become *possible* explanations to the issues of the present, subject to interpretation and personal enactment.

Scholarship concerning native storytelling has strongly emphasized ritual and ceremonial languages, suggesting that the meaning of storytelling comes from the content of a story or its repetitive act. Neglected in such an approach is that the act of storytelling and the context in which stories are shared contribute significantly to the enactment of meaning. Empirical evidence on Kamëntšás' different forms of speech suggests that storytelling functions as much as a constituted symbol as a constituting symbol.

Because I am committed to discussing how meaning reaches completion in narrative experiences and how the act of storytelling is both a constituted and constituting symbol of the quest for meaning, I discuss *bëtaman jenaijabuayan* more extensively than ceremonial or ritual discourse. The reason for this extensive discussion is that *Sayings of the Ancestors* and *So Wise Were Our Elders*, both by McDowell, strongly emphasize the constituted element of storytelling and suggest that the sacred meaning of a story lies not so much in the act of telling but in the content of a story. Neglected in the interpretative work of McDowell is the transformative power of storytelling to the present generation. Using as examples some stories that I have heard, I illustrate how the transformative power of stories leaves the quest for meaning open for discussion, suggesting thereby that the meaning that comes from storytelling is sacredly dynamic, not frozen in time.

i. Storytelling as Constituted Symbol

The two narrative forms that support the claim of storytelling as constituted meaning are the ceremonial and the ritual. While they differ in structure and context, they purport to create meaning through a repetition of the speeches and deeds of the ancestors. Ceremonial speech, *bëtaman jalensensian*, is at present enacted during the most important days of the Kamëntšá culture, during the ascension of the new leader on the first of January of each year, at the end of the Mass in the middle of the annual dancing, and during *Waknaité*, a commemoration of the Day of the Dead.[60] Alberto Juajibioy indicates that the structure of this ceremonial kind of speech resembles the speeches that elders used before social bonding practices, like marriage, baptism, and funeral rites, or even in requesting the help of any other person in any form.[61] The word *bëtaman* denotes ethical and aesthetical meaning, and in ceremonial speech it also means "careful"; *jalensensian* means to have a power to speak. Central to ceremonial language is the idea that one should use the power of language carefully. For example, the youth are often exhorted to speak Kamëntšá with care: "*Bëngbe biyan wamansoy endmën; bošenan jëtsoibuamnayan; ndoñ totsatoibuamná, wenan wuanjaniet*," meaning, "Our language is sacred; we should speak it beautifully, for otherwise it will soon be lost."

A ceremonial speaker starts normally with words like, "*Taita selokbe lisensiá, pamilëpasadangëbe lisensiá, nÿetškangbe lisensiá, atšbe barie tondai merecid, tondai okasionak, ndokarimidi, nÿemo kuentad palabrä respet chëkuasenoperdei. Bëngbe betsëtsang mondbesicham bëngbe waman palabra kuedadok jajuardan.*"[62] Loosely translated it means, "I do not think I deserve at this occasion to speak up, but in the absence of another option, I will somehow be disrespectful in saying a few words."[63] Characteristic of ceremonial language within the Kamëntšá culture is that the speaker is compromised deeply with their immediate audience. Humbly standing before the rest of the universe, the speaker starts reminding the audience that speaking is a sacred act, an endowment that at once ennobles and humbles a person, just like the elders and former leaders had described. Such initial claim is a recognition of the fact that language is a gift of many generations, a crystallization of meaning through time, a testimony of the beginning of a culture. In using ceremonial language, the speaker knows that space and time take a distinctively qualitative aspect that demands personal responsibility, for there is awareness that the conversation takes a sacred dimension, as reflected in the meaning of the expression *waman palabra*, "sacred word." Reflective of this attitude is the speaker's words through which he or she asks permission to the universe, the elders, the former leaders, and the present audience. Ritual and ceremonial language is a form of linking the present community with its roots, with the past. The spiritual forces of the present, the human, the imaginative, and all the temporal and continuous manifestations of existence become intertwined in ceremonial language.

Ritual language is like ceremonial language in that it enacts the speeches of the ancestors and seeks in the past their response for the present. But it differs from ceremonial language in that it is not entirely fixed and in that it functions in a more private context. Ritual language in the Kamëntsá culture takes places in households and functions within healing ceremonies. In *So Wise Were Our Elders*, McDowell quite correctly describes ritual language as the language of native doctors who chant, whistle, and sing to enter the spiritual realm. Because of its ritual character, these performances, says McDowell, "are only partially verbal," meaning that they are not transparently semantic in character.[64] Researcher Omar Alberto Garzón Chiviri characterizes Kamëntsá ritual language as the verbal enactment of the sacred. Based on personal experiences in yajé ceremonies, Garzón Chiviri points out that while the sacred dimension is not fully captured in ritual language, it is fundamental for healing ceremonies, and it is practiced in more private settings.[65]

ii. Scholarship on Storytelling as Constituted Symbol

Records of European travelers crossing over many American lands after the conquest have become primary sources for students of mythology. Most of the famous anthropologists of the twentieth century dedicated to investigating Native American mythology traveled widely and lived with different indigenous peoples or with descendants of ancient native civilizations, and later they published scholarly books that widened the curiosity of intellectuals. American folklorist and ethnomusicologist John Holmes McDowell followed this path in 1978 when he arrived at the Sibundoy Valley and published two books, the first *Sayings of the Ancestors* and then *So Wise Were Our Elders*. In both of these enriching ethnographic books, McDowell interprets the proverbs of the Ingas concerning dream interpretation and the storytelling of the Kamëntsas as following a pattern of constituted, already-made meanings.

McDowell's purpose in *Sayings of the Ancestors* is to account for the spiritual life of the natives of the Sibundoy Valley, with a special emphasis on the spiritual life of the "ordinary" members of the Inga community, shunning the "esoteric kennings" of the ritual specialist.[66] For the purpose of his study, McDowell uses the term "Sibundoy natives" to refer collectively to the indigenous peoples of the valley, drawing freely on the oral traditions of Kamëntšá and Ingas alike, although he mainly discusses two hundred sayings of the Ingas. He argues that the sayings of the ancestors are practical components of a folk religion, "with analogues in many parts of indigenous South America,"[67] which, in functioning as daily orientating beliefs, do not constitute a well-established system of worship. While in some passages, he seems to suggest that the proverbial language of the sayings reveals a dynamic form of spirituality, McDowell prefers to interpret the spiritual life of native Sibundoy in terms of foundational spiritual forces that have remained intact over the years.

In *Sayings of the Ancestors*, McDowell characterizes the spiritual realm as the grounding of the sayings from the beginning times and as the primordial constraining source of spirituality in the valley. He says that those spiritual forces "alert people to the insistent activity in the spirit realm, which constantly threatens to wreak havoc in the fragile course of human lives."[68] And he adds that "the sayings conserve fidelity to the example of the first people, who established for all time the guidelines for a civilized life."[69] The well-being of the community, in McDowell's interpretation, depends on "aligning the contemporary frame of events with this eternal ancestral model."[70] The expression "saying of the ancestors" comes from the Inga expression *nugpa-manda-cuna imasa rima-sca-cuna*, which McDowell translated as "how the first people used to speak."[71] *The Inga Language* by Stephen H. Levinsohn suggests that the prefix *ñuj* indicates old times, but not necessarily primordial times. A dictionary on Inga language published in 1997 also suggests that *Ñugpamanda* is an adjective or adverb to refer to *lo antiguo, lo anterior, lo de antes, lo pasado*, "the old times,"[72] all of which not necessarily indicating a beginning in time, but only indicating a temporal dimension of meaning. Levinsohn transcribes the story of a powerful dragon who used to devour elected Inga peoples. This is the beginning of the story: "*Ñujpátaca domingocuna suj sug gentesi cacharinacug rirca. dragon canchis umayuj canchis chupayujsi llujsicurca cada domingo micungapa tragangapa*," which, as translated by Levinsohn, means, "In olden times on Sundays they used to choose people out, one at a time, and hand them over. A dragon with seven heads and seven tails used to come out every Sunday to eat and devour." The story goes on, saying that the dragon would wipe out the entire Inga population unless a man to be devoured would be handed to him every Sunday; the Ingas of the old times used to choose the victims among those who did not go to Mass. At least in colloquial Inga language, the expression

Ñujpátaca means old times and does not refer to the beginnings of all times. In the story of the dragon here referred, old times does not refer to the beginning of time. On the contrary, the story refers to the times when the Ingas had incorporated Catholic teachings into their lives, which, of course, does not mark the beginning of the times of the Inga peoples.

In equating *nugpamanda* with a primordial people and suggesting that a group of first people set an exemplary mode of life that became "a cultural treasure, passed from one generation to another since the beginning,"[73] McDowell disregards the syncretic and dynamic elements of the spirituality of the proverbs and their temporally constructed meanings. Quite clearly, he says that "in spite of the devout efforts of many generations of Catholic missionaries, these Andean Indians continue to believe that a timeless truth was established by the first ancestors." He writes,

> At every turn the sayings exalt the example of the ancestors, who are viewed as spiritually far superior to the modern people. The underlying notion can be conceived of as a Sibundoy equivalent to the big-bang theory, premised on a pivotal instant in cosmic history that determines for *all time the shape and meaning of all things to come*. This pivotal moment is the dawn of human civilization, when the celestial bodies interacted directly with the first people, when the line between animals and people was yet to be drawn, and when the coalescence of brute spiritual power set in motion the forces that created the natural and social universes of contemporary human experience [emphasis added].[74]

While thought-provoking, such an account appears partly groundless. The claim that Inga ancestors are viewed as far superior by modern Ingas speaks adequately of how newer generations of natives look to their elders in the quest for meaning. The claim that a primordial outburst of spiritual force determines for "all time the shape and meaning of all things" to come does not seem well-justified. The sociocultural transformation that stirs the creative spirit of the natives of Sibundoy indicates that some stories and sayings function as *possible* explanations of present events, not as dogmatic systems. Historical, linguistic, and ethnographic research further suggests that the Ingas, travelers and traders as they were, have remained in contact with several other travelers, adopting and changing parts of their culture and their spirituality, even before the arrival of the Spaniards. To assume that the spiritual life of the Ingas has remained unaffected since the beginning of time, stored sacredly in "an unbroken chain of transmission . . . making it available to those who are clever enough to profit from its warnings,"[75] is, objectively speaking, at least difficult to imagine.

In other passages of the same book, *Saying of the Ancestors*, McDowell's interpretation of the primordial spiritual force looks ambiguous. Despite the thesis of the primacy of an original, pristine spiritual force at the beginning of time in the Inga culture, some of McDowell's assertions suggest that the sayings are expressions of a dynamic spirituality. Statements like, "It would be a mistake to take the sayings as empty holdovers from a previous belief system,"[76] or passages like, "The Sibundoy natives have indeed absorbed much from the European and mestizo cultures that have so profoundly altered their historical destiny,"[77] illustrate that the spiritual realm that orients the daily life of the present natives is dynamic and in process of reinvention. As he himself declares, "The flexibility within the content of the traditional code favors a creative adaptation to particular circumstances,"[78] and "by virtue of the flexibility that resides in the sayings themselves . . . people manage to adapt the abstract code of the sayings to the practical realities of their lives."[79] Other passages, however, demonstrate an opposite thesis.

McDowell believes that the collection of two hundred proverbs of the Inga peoples that he documents, and which resemble Kamëntšá proverbs, is the efficient effect of a primary, grounding spiritual force. The Inga expression for dreams is *muscuycunamanda,* or "concerning dreams,"[80] and the Kamëntšá expression is *otjenayama.*[81] In McDowell's interpretation, the present world, in which the natives of Sibundoy are the effect of a primordial spiritual realm, its existence and meaning, depends ultimately on adequately interpreting the deeds of the ancestors back at the beginning of time. Neglected in such a deterministic approach is the creative power of Ingas and Kamëntšás to understand their own historical circumstances and to imagine that its cultural references do not come from the beginning of time.

One of the sayings that is common in the two native groups in Sibundoy refers to dream interpretation concerning cows, priests, and nuns. Take as examples the interpretations of dreams that refer to cows. The expression *"Huagra muscuchimi huayra yucahura,"* in Inga, meaning, "when you are dreaming cows you are sick because of bad spirits,"[82] and the Kamëntšá saying, *"Oveshá, uacná, bachnë or madrá tcojtsotjená, ana bacná binÿe jtsatsjanjama,"* meaning, "if one dreams sheep, cows, priests, or nuns, one will be sick of bad winds,"[83] suggest not a primordial original force, but a creative interpretation of dreams. As McDowell himself comments, "Dream images of cow, horse, or auto, reflects [*sic*] the alienation of the indigenous population from these animals and artifacts introduced by the Spanish missionaries or Colombian colonos [white people]."[84] The changing interpretation of dreams clearly is an indication that there is a creative impulse in rendering the experience of dreaming meaningful and contextually dynamic.

Sayings of the Ancestors concludes with a framework to interpret the narratives of the natives of Sibundoy in terms of the unfolding of a primordial spiritual force that gradually loses its efficacy in modern times. In this gradual process of decay of spiritual power, "contemporary events are viewed as pale reflections of their ancestral prototypes" because "the spiritual forces that guided the creation of the world and the establishment of human society . . . were active in their most dramatic form during these earlier moments in the cosmic time sequence."[85] This gradual degradation of spiritualty, according to McDowell, is present in the Kamëntsás and Ingas alike. In a self-critical moment of his writings, McDowell asks, "How far back can we trace the wellsprings of the ancestral world?" To this question, he answers that it is unlikely to find the primordial original myths because each older generation carries some part of the story to the grave. He adds to this difficulty the fact that Catholic missionaries assiduously sought the extirpation of the native religion.[86] But despite such an explicit recognition that the primordial spiritual force might not be as apparent as he wants it to be, McDowell believes that it is possible to offer a mythological interpretation of the native storytelling as practiced in the Sibundoy Valley. Following a story shared with him by Bautista Juajibioy, a Kamëntsá elder, McDowell concludes *Saying of the Ancestors* with two hypotheses: first, there is a clear story that suggests an evolution of the culture, from a raw time to a time of fire. And second, he argues for a distinctive, culturally embodied cosmology with temporal subdivisions: primordial (marked by the raw time and the time of fire), ancestral (wherein stories narrate human cooperation with animals), and modern times (wherein the spiritual life takes the form of Christianity).

McDowell backs up his hypothesis of the raw time and the time of fire[87] with a story in which a weasel goes to steal the fire from Wangëtsmen. Except for minor changes, the version here presented is like McDowell's:

> When there was no fire, people used to eat raw. One day as they were complaining about not having fire, a weasel showed up and said: "I promise to get you fire if each of you gives me a chicken in return: if you don't assent to such an offer, I won't do you this favor." When they thought it over, the people agreed to the deal. Then the weasel went to the home of Wangëtsmen because only he had the fire. As she entered his house, she said, "Sir, should I make you laugh?" He answered, "OK, make me laugh." Then the weasel started to dance, moving her tail over the ground. Suddenly she approached the fire, took cinders with her tail, ran out from the place quickly, went to the forest, and spread the cinders over there. Instantly those places caught fire. On seeing this, the people went out immediately to pick up fire. Since this time there is fire in this place. The mice taught about corn planting. Fortitude also came about to this place from this time.[88]

As McDowell correctly points out, the previous story is foundational to the Kamëntsá culture in that it explains the evolution of a culture. Fire in the story is at once the symbol of a new time and of a new way of life; the concluding segment of the story suggests that fortitude came into being with fire and corn. Yet, the problem with McDowell's account of the experience of native storytelling of the Sibundoy Valley is that he interprets the rest of the mythology not in the context of meaning within the community but in terms of categorical interpretations that provide theoretical meaning to scholars but not to native communities. The idea that there is a cultural hero, Wangëtsmen, and all native stories become meaningful as they relate the deeds of this cultural hero is problematic for two reasons. First, the only story in which Wangëtsmen is explicitly mentioned is the story of the weasel that robs fire. I have asked all the elders of my family, and none has given me any account of Wangëtsmen. It might be suggested that this is not a sufficient reason, for after all, even McDowell wrote that "the Kamsá people have mostly lost contact with their culture hero, Wangetsmuna, though for the moment they continue to value a generalized concept of the 'ancestors' and to locate an abiding communal investment in tales about these influential first people."[89] It is very significant that only by assuming that McDowell's view of the unfolding of a founding spiritual force at the beginning of time can one imagine the existence of *a* cultural hero that actualizes the pure potentiality of that primordial spiritual force. And it is also significant that it would be *a* cultural hero in a community that is socially, politically, and morally organized in terms of councils. Second, had my two-previous generations of ancestors forgotten to speak of our "cultural founding father," Wangëtsmen, it is yet difficult to assert why they have stopped retelling stories of a cultural hero and a father. In all publications on Kamëntsá and Inga stories, in all written and oral documentations I have accessed, Wangëtsmen is explicitly mentioned only once, in the story of the weasel who steals fire above referred. Despite this empirical evidence, McDowell interprets all the native storytelling as the unfolding of a primordial spiritual force that takes a new dimension with the cultural hero and reaches a degrading form in contemporary times.

So Wise Were Our Elders follows the same general line of argumentation that he proposed in *Sayings of the Ancestors*, except that it is dedicated to the narrative experiences of the Kamëntsá people. Like in his previous book on the proverb-like Inga sayings, in *So Wise* McDowell states, "Kamsá mythic narrative exists within the framework of a Sibundoy Big-bang theory of cultural evolution, a theory that explicates all subsequent history in relation to the pivotal example of the first people. . . . The myths tell not only of the eradication and subduing of adverse spiritual presences, but also of the loss of an intended earthly paradise."[90] Because he is committed to sustaining a sharp distinction between mythology and folktale, McDowell finds it difficult to think that experiences of storytelling, which require personal engagement, might be of mythical character. Listening to and recording one of his informants, he writes, "Maria Juajibioy concentrates on the moments of conflict between story protagonists. She is drawn to the emotional and dramatic core of the stories, and her performances are more personalized, less imbued with cosmological detail, than those of the other narrators. I see them as moving in the direction of folktale, yet she too expressed a conviction that the events she narrated really did happen in the days of the ancestors."[91]

McDowell equates myth with unwavering religious truths. He writes that a myth is a sacred story that narrates explicitly or implicitly religious beliefs and practices. Myths offer a vision of life and the cosmos at large, and they lose their spiritual power when they become legends or stories for instruction: "The myths of the Kamsá people retain a religious function, particularly as embodiments of ancestral wisdom, but they are evolving toward a folktale corpus as entertainment and moral instruction take precedence over the manifestation of religious truth."[92] This loss of religious force leads McDowell to suggest that myths gradually lose efficacy. "The adjectival form, 'mythic,'" writes McDowell "signals a dissolution of myth's essence." And he adds, "Kamsá mythic narrative presents a mythology in transition, one that might well take on the appearance of a folktale corpus as the community becomes increasingly less connected to its traditional cosmology. The present narrative corpus possesses attributes of both myth and folktale, thought I would argue that it tilts for the moment in the direction of myth."[93] In partial disagreement with Stith Thomson's statement that an exact delimitation between myth and legend remains fruitless,[94] and with a strong agreement with Erminie Voegelin's view that divine actors make mythical narratives while human actors constitute legends and tales, McDowell states that "mythology is imbued with actual religious precept and that folktale and legend are secular in character."[95] Holding this distinction, in 1998 before the Symposium on Andean Studies at Bloomington, Indiana, McDowell presented the same conclusion, saying that Kamëntšá's narrative is either personal or mythical.[96] The personal narrative more relates an individual's encounter with the divine, and the mythical refers more to the stories that take the individual in question to the time of his or her ancestors.

McDowell is not alone in interpreting native storytelling in terms of myths and legends.[97] In both *The Sacred and the Profane* and *The Myth of the Eternal Return*, Mircea Eliade expressed his idea of myth as a true story of the creation of the real and the founding of the spiritual power. He also characterized legends as stories with less efficacy than myths. "Myth," he wrote, "narrates a sacred history; it relates an event that took place in primordial Time, the fabled time of the 'beginnings.'" And he clarified his view saying that "myth tells how, through the deeds of Supernatural Beings, a reality came into existence, be it the whole of reality, the Cosmos, or only a fragment of reality. . . . Myth, then, is always an account of a 'creation'; it relates how something was produced, began to be."[98] In Eliade's interpretation, people of primitive societies understood themselves in a relation so intimate with the rest of the universe that they did not think of themselves as autonomous or independent beings. In *The Myth of the Eternal Return*, he wrote that in the general behavior of archaic man, we can see that "neither the objects of the external world nor human acts, properly speaking, have any autonomous intrinsic value. . . . The object appears as the receptacle of an exterior force that differentiates it from its milieu and gives it meaning and value."[99] The archaic man, he said, "acknowledges no act which has not been previously posited and lived by someone else, some other being who was not a man. What he does has been done before. His life is the ceaseless repetition of gestures initiated by others."[100] This characterization, perhaps true of some societies that Eliade studied, misrepresents the experience of storytelling among the Kamëntšá and Inga people. To be sure, the content of some of the stories that one hears in Sibundoy suggests the dramatic transformation of individuals in the face of spiritual powers. But those stories do not suggest total alienation of the creative spirit of natives nor do they suggest that stories founded all human behavior. Far from being profane, stories of elders who journey and were endowed with visions to heal new diseases are common both among Kamëntšá and Inga medical doctors. These cultural manifestations suggest living elements of creativity that do not follow the logic of sharp distinction between myth and legends. Against his insistence that the sayings of the ancestors or the stories of the Kamëntšás reveal a pattern of mythic thinking like Eliade suggested, McDowell's ethnographic evidence suggests that the spiritual life of the Sibundoy Valley was sacredly dynamic.

iii. Storytelling as Constituting Symbol

It was William James and John Dewey who indicated that intellectuals tend to apply, at times forcefully, conceptual references of past experiences to new forms of living experiences that could be more nuanced than a theory would suggest. James called this a psychological fallacy, and Dewey called it the philosophical fallacy. McDowell made a similar mistake. Like many anthropologists doing research on native cultures, McDowell committed an anthropological fallacy in as much as his interpretative books seek to prove that the narrative experiences of native peoples remain devoid of creativity and innovation and are bound by former times. Storytelling is not significant because one shares the *same* old story. A significant part of the meaning of the stories in native cultures depends on the transformative effect that the act of telling a story brings in a specific context. To listen to voices of the ancestors and their deeds implies a shared history and the responsibility of imagining the possibility of a common destiny. As they are crystalized forms of a living culture, they exert a powerful transformative effect on the audience, creating a special aura of meaning to present and future generations. In implicitly neglecting the transformative power of native stories, McDowell takes it for granted that native cultures remain frozen in time.

Because he links the value of a story with its content, McDowell disregards the personally transforming power of a story. Neglected in McDowell's interpretation is that the voice of the storyteller creates an aura of significance that shapes the content of a narrated story and that spurs the audience's imagination into thinking of the meaning of life as an open quest.

Following Royce, Peirce, Dewey and Mead, in *The Human Eros*, Thomas M. Alexander offers a philosophy of culture that provides better theoretical equipment to understand the interpretative process of meaning creation in native narratives across generations, indicating that our human existence is driven by a desire to experience life with a sense of meaning and value.[101] The absence of meaning and value turns cultures on the path of self-destruction. Alexander describes cultures as living, as "spiritual ecologies" that respond to the quest for meaning, their constituted core narratives in which meanings are expressed as "mythos," the specific determination of mythos as "tropes," and the clusters of mutual cultural references in which tropes relate to one another as "constellations." Using this framework, one can see that core stories provide meaning using different symbolic elements. Dances, rituals, and stories, for example, enact core beliefs and provide a line of continuity to the living cultures.

Central to Alexander's philosophy is that cultures, as spiritual ecologies that answer to the quest for meaning, are living systems[102] in the sense that they do not take the past as causal conditions for the present, but as "one interpretative horizon constituting the present,"[103] and the future as the other interpretative horizon that constitutes the present. Following the works of Josiah Royce, Alexander characterizes the interpretative horizon of the past as the community of memory and the interpretative horizon of the future as the community of hope. The community that asserts the narrative meanings of its past does not simply repeat the teachings of ancestors but seeks to engage in the very process of meaning creation. The act of telling a story in Kamëntsá or Inga is an act of engagement in the process of meaning creation. Because cultures crystalize meanings based on their past and on their expectations, the living experiences of communities are always dynamic; their individuals engage in genuine acts of communication and interpretation in which dialogical spaces become explorations of possibilities of meaning creation.[104] Following Professor Alexander's outlines for a philosophy of culture and his idea of cultures as spiritual ecologies that create, interpret, and imagine meaningful ways of living, one can conclude that a significant portion of the Kamëntsá and Inga storytelling experiences is disregarded when the meaning of stories is strictly tied to their content, as McDowell suggested.

My interpretation of storytelling as a symbolic temporal dimension of a culture is not new. Written meditations on the experiences of native North American storytelling, as described by N. Scott Momaday and Thomas King,[105] suggest also that the act of telling a story is as fundamental as the content of the story in the creation of meaning. Characterizing storytelling as the oldest and the most refined of the human forms of crystallizing meaning out of existence, Kiowa storyteller Momaday wrote that in an oral tradition, "words and the things that are made of words are tentative," adding that "a song, or a prayer, or a story, is always but one generation removed from extinction."[106] Reflecting on native North American traditions, Momaday indicated that in oral traditions, we develop a different attitude to language and to life itself. Words are chosen carefully in oral traditions, and neither they nor our existence is taken for granted.[107] This is as much true of native North America as it is of native South America. "We should always be careful in what we tell ourselves," my grandfather used to say when I became an adult. Using as example his agricultural skills, he used to tell me that words of wisdom are as difficult to cultivate as corn in winter. Like my grandfather, Momaday is fully aware of the fact that one takes a different attitude to language and existence when one lives primarily in an oral tradition in which Time takes a special consideration.

Storytellers in oral traditions know that the bounds of sisterhood and the sense of relationship with the rest of Nature might be at risk if words are chosen carelessly. While limited by the life experiences of the community of the storytellers, words in oral traditions have power to intensify, create, or ruin the sense of beauty, truth, and the holy; as Momaday says, "One who has only an oral tradition thinks of language in this way: my words exist at the level of my voice. If I do not speak with care, my words are wasted. If I do not listen with care, words are lost. If I do not remember carefully, the very purpose of words is frustrated."[108] Using *Black Elk Speaks* as an example of the native North American storytelling tradition, Momaday says Black Elk, through the intercession of John Neihardt, takes it upon himself to speak formally and creatively, assuming the responsibility for his words. Black Elk, says Momaday, is careful not to intrude upon the story because the story is not essentially autobiographical, but a testament of a life that transcends the physical horizon.

Momaday not only reflects on storytelling. He is a storyteller and thus is aware of his consistency and responsibility in using language. In *The Way to Rainy Mountain*, Momaday masters the art of storytelling in three different voices that recount the experience of storytelling from the Native Americans' view. The first voice speaks of the crystalized meaning of the oldest times, of the memory of older generations. This is the voice of the farthest past that comes to the present in the act of telling a story. The second voice is more personal and brings in the feeling of a present generation that imaginatively takes up its presentness; this is the voice that converses with close relatives. It is the testimony of the voice of the storyteller that sees his or her immediate present in the light of his or her inherited creative spirit. Finally, it is the voice of a historian, of the one who believes it is possible to write one's past somehow detachedly. While it might look foreign, the voice of the historian has the power to shape the voice of the storyteller, and thus it demands more creativity from the storyteller. From these three voices one learns that the present demands more creativity than the past. These three voices are not disruptive but constitute acts of engagement with the present, past, and future, and they function as dynamic forces that demand more creative answers in the quest for meaning. As one engages in the journey to *Rainy Mountain* and moves from one story to the next, one experiences that Momaday's writing style is not fortuitous. On the contrary, one notices that his is a testimony of the *act* of storytelling.

Momaday's personal awareness suggests that the act of telling a story is at least as significant as the content of the story. Echoing the words of Momaday, in *The Truth about Stories*, Thomas King explains that storytellers in Native American experiences have a power to control lives; he says, "I tell the stories not to play on your sympathies but to suggest how stories can control our lives, for there is a part of me that has never been able to move past these stories, a part of me that will be chained to these stories as long as I live."[109] Like Momaday, King is aware that native storytelling in North America demands an awareness of history, of the present, and of the future. Imaginatively, he describes the act of telling stories as an engagement with meaning.

Approaches like Momaday's to the experience of native storytelling contrast with McDowell, Eliade, and Cassirer, or with any of the intellectuals that trace sharp distinctions between the meaning of storytelling based upon the content of a narrative and the meaning that comes from the act of telling a story. Linking the fibers of memory and imagination, of time and space, the transformative effect of storytelling remains at the heart of Native American consciousness, individually and collectively. The spirit of the voices of the ancestors has always been a fundamental part of the Native American experience. A careful listening to a Kamëntšá elder, to his or her most intimate life experience as revealed in his voice and language, suggests that the sacredness of a story in these lands of Sibundoy is dynamic, responding to the circumstances of the community. Naturally, the attitude of the storyteller changes when confronted with a person who asks about the story for the sake of investigation and curiosity rather than with a child or a growing adult seeking advice in life.

A kind of intimacy on the part of the storyteller is lost when he or she is forced to perform a story for another person who from the beginning takes it to be more relevant to classify theoretically stories as "sacred" or "profane." Careful as they are while sharing a story, all storytellers in the Sibundoy Valley know that the act of telling is transformative in that it creates meaning. To tell a story is not to report a past event; storytellers know that stories have the potential power of transforming present and future generations.

The construction of meaning for human life in Sibundoy does not depend on axiomatically following the primordial energies of the universe, but in having a resilient capacity to interpret imaginatively the present and the future. Stories remain true in the mind in the sense that they give continuity to the process of value-formation and value-orientation of former times, not in the sense that they provide the meaning of all things to come. When one is engaged with the stories of the elders, one can feel that the voices of the ancestors come to the present as suggestions.

In addition to the ceremonial and ritual language, present in the Kamëntsá culture is the familiar and the communal kind of speech. While the expression *bëtaman jacuentan* denotes familiar speeches and the expression *bëtaman jenoiunayan* means communal speech, both could be translated as "let's have meaningful conversations." Except for the location where they are shared, these two forms of speeches aim at educating morally and aesthetically. *Bëtaman jacuentan* is practiced at home and *bëtaman jeyoiunayan* takes place in communal works, in *mingas* and *cuadrillas*. At present still in practice in some parts of Sibundoy, a *minga* is a form of collective work wherein one works for a person in exchange for food and drinks. *Cuadrillas* used to be more business-oriented forms of collective work in which some money might be negotiated. While young adults and adults could join cuadrillas or mingas freely, one's membership used to be more permanent in a cuadrilla than in a minga. A minga was more an ad hoc workgroup for one day and lacked the leadership of the cuadrillas. At present virtually extinct, a cuadrilla used to be a common practice to gain work experience; it was, so to speak, an internship into the lifework of a farm.[110]

In the context of having meaningful conversations, Kamëntsá storytellers do not claim to be the owners of stories. Their acts of telling, although they might refer to past actions, aim at educating for the present and the future. The act of telling a story is an act of constant potentiality, for the meaning is not exhausted in the content of the story, but in the fact that it is shared in a specific context. Both moral and aesthetic education is central in the familiar and communal kinds of Kamëntsá speeches, and the unfolding of a story goes along with agricultural or artistic activities. On farms, children and young adults learn of the challenges of life through the development of stories. One of my favorite farm stories is the story of "Francisco, the One of the Trousers." I heard the story in a *minga* at my father's farm when we were doing the last of the three weedings to the corn field. The story goes as follows:

> People say that there used to live a native man named Francisco who traveled to the city of Pasto to trade corn and fruits. A normal trip would take him three days, one day walking, a day for the business, and one day to get back to the town. Once Francisco decided to stay in Pasto for a week and a half. For some

unknown reason he had decided to change his clothes and look like a white. Instead of wearing a cusma, a sayo, and a belt, as the men of the time usually did, he came back to the town wearing pants, shoes, and a shirt. On his return, he had brought more of those clothes to wear regularly. Nobody had ever imagined that Francisco would become the laughingstock of the community. People used to make fun of other people because they would work tirelessly with no reason other than to be busy, and in general people would relax if others were not working as crazy as they did. But Francisco had taken the meaning of being funny to another level. He had demonstrated that one could be funny and not be deterred by others. It looked like his clothes had changed his spirit, as he did not seem to be bothered that some of his closest friends wanted to learn more Spanish just to pretend that they could address Francisco in the proper manner, saying, "Buenos días, Señor Francisco." Because he felt uncomfortable, Francisco eventually dressed like the old days, but it somehow was too late, as everyone already called him Francisco, the gentleman of the trousers. We could probably continue to make fun of him even though we all at present look like Francisco.

Humorous stories that describe cultural transformation are not unusual in Sibundoy in communal work. In addition to entertaining the audience, communal stories provide powerful moral lessons. The end of the story is an invitation to think about the meaning of the story. While the story remains funny, it suggests that the laughingstock of the community might be the community of the present and that the once humorous story might now be bittersweet. Implicit in the recognition that today we all look like Francisco is a recognition that the generation of the present is at once the subject and the object of humor. The story of Francisco typifies the kind of story that serves as a lesson of the past that should be considered in the present. Like in ceremonial or ritual language, the communal kind of language demands responsibility from the speaker, even if the story to be shared is humorous.

In households one typically hears stories that respond to personal, more intimate concerns. When I was a child, I used to wake up at the sound of thunder and became scared of lighting. One night I was helping my mom to thresh corn grains while she was waving sashes and making *bëkoy* (maize beer). When I asked her if she knew about the rays, she told me this story:

> A widower living with his two children decided to marry another woman. The new wife disliked the kids and used not to feed them. One day the widower decided to take his kids to the mountain and make a new house for them out there. The children agreed and when the stepmother was still sleeping, the three of them grabbed plenty of corn and left home. Before entering the mountain, the father told his kids: "Please wait for me here until you hear a rhythmic sound of my ax cutting a trunk, like the one you hear when I cut the wood for a bonfire; then, walk through the hallmarks of corn grain until you find me." Hopeful, the children waited.

As it was noon and no sound came out yet, the siblings decided to walk following the corn hallmark. Suddenly, a beautiful, natural sound, followed by another, and another, like the one expected, burst out in the hill. Happily, they followed the sound, their hearts full of hope. Sadly, soon they realized that the sound came from the collision of two pumpkins from gusts of wind. Neither father nor house was out there.

Darkness was falling slowly upon the hill when they saw a little smoke billowing at a distance. Thinking that their dad had made it, the children walked toward the smoke. Soon they saw it coming from a nice, beautiful cottage, of the kind of beauty unseen before, with open doors and glass dispensers with fried meat and fresh corn cakes at the entrance, enticing the children to come in. Curious and adventurous, the two agreed that the boy should rob while the girl would remain on guard. It might've been funny to have seen the shy brother acting like a cat catching mice, for the initial silent moment soon became a gust of shared laughter.

A very old woman spoke from inside the house and stopped the joyfulness. Asking them to call her "Dear Grandmother," she invited them to eat as they pleased, saying not to worry for their father because he had been taking care of her illness. "Eat as you please," she told them, adding, "then please help me to collect water and make a fire." When the siblings had eaten as they pleased, they started with the chores. While collecting water, they noticed that the head of their slain father was in a large pot. The two spoke quietly and planned to escape. They decided to put a lot of dry wood in the fire to make the water boil faster. Once the water was about to boil, they planned to turn the fire off and to pretend to not know how to turn it on. Showing frustration and kindness, they then would beg the old woman to teach them about the art of fire blowing. As this old woman lay close to the fire, the children threw the boiling water on her and ran away down the hill, just as they had planned.

Darkness had almost covered the hill when the siblings ran into a river and met a man sharpening his ax. On hearing their story, the man told them he would help them only if they promised him not to be scared and to remain still on the other side of the river when the old woman came. He said to them that he would pretend to help her too, but as she would be crossing over the river, the bridge would fall apart. As the children agreed, the man jumped into the river and turned himself into a bridge. Once the children crossed the river, the bridge vanished, and the man appeared again on the other side.

After a few minutes, the old woman came in, swearing that she would punish them. When she asked the man for help, the man jumped into the river and became a bridge. As the woman was crossing in the middle, the bridge broke apart and the woman fell into the river, turning herself into a half-woman-half-frog creature. Still capable of revenge, the woman got herself out of the river and continued to chase the children.

Darkness covered the hill almost entirely when the children met another man who was sitting quietly. The siblings begged him for help, and he hid them under the bench. As the frog-woman came, the man took the children in his arms, tossed them up in the air. They become lightning rays and the woman-frog had no option other than to accept her nature and cry forever before the night's lightning.

My mom told me that she heard this story from her mom who in turn heard it from her mom. As a child I used to keep this story as a secret when I was scared at night; thinking of the courage of the two children, I imagined I could one day face challenges with a similar attitude. It took me a while to understand that the meaning of the story does not lie in its content, but in the fact that my mom gave it to me. Later in my life I learned that on hearing stories like these, one comes to realize the meaning of the immediate relation that human life has with the rest of the universe, however one imagines its ultimate components to be. The story of the origins of the lightning rays at present reminds me that my existence participates in a meaningful narrative process with the elders and with the rest of the universe as I experience it today. I participate in the feeling of relatedness that the elders learned to establish with the natural world. In giving me the story, my mom made me aware that the meaning of my existence lies in my capacity to understand my life in relation to my ancestors and the rest of the universe.

The voice of the storyteller is a bridge that connects us more intimately with our past and reorients our being as we come back to the present. Stories tell us not of solidified events but of living forces that coexist within us. With them we know that the past is a living force of our present and that we participate in a constant flow of time. They are the voices of our being.

III. CONCLUSION

The meaning of storytelling for Kamëntsá people does not depend on the theoretical distinction between myth and folklore as McDowell has suggested in his books. McDowell has considered the experience of storytelling in the Sibundoy Valley only partially, emphasizing its constituted meanings, but has altogether disregarded its constituting meanings. In as much as he has interpreted the sayings of the Inga peoples as the remnants of a pristine spiritual force and the stories of the Kamëntsá as the expression of myth in the sense of an unchanged spiritual narrative, he has only considered storytelling in terms of constituted meaning, that is, in terms of ceremonial and ritual language. And he has ignored the dynamic interpretive forms of speech, the *bëtaman jenoiunayan*, which provide a framework to interpret storytelling in terms of creative, suggestive meanings of life for the present and the future of the people who participate in those stories.

It might be claimed that my criticisms of Professor McDowell are anachronistic, that I am criticizing a work on ethnography of the late 1970s. I have no better answer other than to say that his ethnographic research and the life experience of the generation that he interviewed suggest a different reading, one that takes more seriously the life experiences of the people involved in the tradition of storytelling, that is, the life experiences of those affected by the continuous narratives and who tell the story not because they are in front of someone who is investigating but in front of their own challenges. In as much as I have personally heard the stories with the explicit purpose of creating meaning for new generations in the face of challenging situations, I cannot agree with McDowell's hypothesis.

The experiences that I am relating do not necessarily reflect my idiosyncratic character. Experiences of other native storytellers confirm my hypothesis that the attitude, voice, and purpose of the storyteller in transmitting to the audience a meaning of existence on which he or she has meditated are as important as the content of the story. As I have here demonstrated, both Momaday and Thomas King have written extensively of their experiences as native storytellers. I have also suggested that at present we are endowed with suggestive ideas about culture, like the one espoused by Professor Alexander, which views cultures as living ecologies that actualize and reinterpret their presentness in the light of the past and the future and not as mere entities that almost blindly reproduce or repeat their past.

The absence of categories like *myth* or *folklore* in Kamëntšá culture does not mean that there is no possible theorization about their narrative experiences. The category of storytelling, or "bëtaman jenoiunayan," meaning "sharing meaningful conversations," at the same time the oldest form of cultural survival and the most revealing element of cultural loss, suffices to comprehend the constituting meaning of the narrative experiences. *Bëtaman jenoiunayan*, or storytelling, takes us back to the times when no electricity meant to my ancestors more time to enjoy the clarity of the new moon, more time to bind themselves in the seeking of collective meanings of existence. At present Kamëntšá and Inga stories condense the meanings of memorable experiences of many generations. My parents heard stories from their parents, who in turn heard them from their grandparents. This practice of passing stories forms a web of core beliefs that attempt to keep the whole community alive. Our Kamëntšá storytellers have taken up the fragility of human voice, showing that without a story, our qualitative experience of time could vanish into nothingness. Aware of the fact that language is at once our best-shared tool to make sense of our existence and our best way of leading ourselves astray, Kamëntšá storytellers compromise themselves in telling a story. Knowing that their words have consequences for their audiences, they painstakingly choose words, depending on the audience. In addition to offering moral guidance and at times providing entertainment, Kamëntšá storytelling foremost aims at creating a form of unifying collective sense, one in which the internal or subjective aspect of experiencing the world and seeing it as meaningful coalesces with the external or objective forces that have constrained the spiritual life of the culture.

All storytellers know that they must make difficult decisions in telling one or another story. Asking permission to the elders before giving a speech signifies that there is a responsibility to oneself, to a story, and to an audience. This form of speech, proper of ritual and ceremonial language, suggests that there is a form of constituted meaning that orients the present. But at the same time, those stories have proven to be transformative in the act of telling.

Writing some of the stories referenced here brought me a bittersweet experience. The meaning of words resurrected old experiences, bringing them fully alive again, despite my writing in a foreign language. I often felt like living the same experiences twice, my dreams taking me to the beautiful times, my nightmares forcing me to keep writing until I would purge myself from difficult experiences. Notwithstanding the quality of the experiences I related previously, my writing made them more significant. But once I finished describing them, a feeling of doubt grew again; a kind of faint skepticism on my word choice would suddenly turn into a self-questioning experience, asking myself if I was destroying all my good memories in the very process of writing them and about them. I have found solace in remembering that my analysis of storytelling here presented is a deliberate process of value-formation of the narrative experiences of my own culture. Any judgment on the experience of storytelling must rest on the meaning that stories might have for human life. Native stories are living memories of many generations. They are suggestive of how human life seeks an answer to the quest for meaning, not cultural proofs of the unfolding of an absolute truth. In bringing up the stories of my culture that remain most significant to me, I have unavoidably embodied the personal dimension that is fundamental in any storytelling experience. Behind a native story, there is always the feeling of a generation that speaks of its past, its present, and its future.

NOTES

1. This symbolic meaning is frequently expressed as follows: "*Los indígenas hemos tomado la tierra simbólicamente como la madre, de ella depende nuestra existencia material y guardamos a ella el respeto sagrado, porque es ella parte de la naturaleza y a la vez maestra del mismo hombre*" [We the indigenous [Kamëntšás] have taken the land symbolically as the mother, as our material existence depends on her. We respect her in the sacred way, because she is part of the whole nature and at the same time the teacher of the very human being].Documento Communidad Camëntšá, *Procesos de Tranformación y Alternativas de Autgestión Indígena* (Bogotá: Editorial ABC 1989), 20. I discuss more extensively these senses of land in chapter 3 of this work.

2. Political leaders of the community still greet the community using these words. Alberto Juajibioy Chindoy offers some examples of formal ways of talking: "A Dios lastema. Kach nÿetšá Diosbe lwar chebunjiyalesentsiá [In front of God I humble myself to greet you again]." Cfr. Alberto Juajibioy, *Lenguaje Ceremonial y Narraciones Tradicionales de la Cultura Kamëntšá* (México City: Fondo de Cultura Económica, 2008), 28.

3. Diagnostico Plan Salvaguarda, *Sboachan Jtabouashëntsam Natjëmban Nÿestkang Jtsyëñëngam: Sembrando el Maíz, Fruto de la Fuerza y la Esperanza para asegurar el Buen Vivir Camëntšá* (Sibundoy: Cabildo Indígena Camëntšá Ministerio del Interior, 2012), 30.

4. Indicating that we pay too little attention to the gradual loss of indigenous cultures, Wade Davis suggested that we should see in native languages the condensed forms of interpret-

ing reality differently. He wrote, "More than a cluster of words or a set of grammatical rules, a language is a flash of the human spirit, the filter through which the soul of each particular culture reaches into the material world." Cfr. Wade Davis, *Light at the Edge of the World: A Journey through the Realm of Vanishing Cultures* (Vancouver: Douglas and McIntyre, 2007), 6.

    5. Melvin Lee Bristol, "Sibundoy Ethnobotany" (PhD diss., Harvard University, 1965), 7–8.

    6. Ibid., 19. Bristol provides photographic evidence of these terraces, but he says that when he asked the elders about them in 1965, the natives he spoke with did not provide any explanation.

    7. Numerous accounts of Carlos Tamabioy have been reported. Just when the Capuchin missionaries had started, Miguel Triana traveled the south of Colombia and wrote how whites were taking possession of the native lands. He wrote: "De tiempo atrás, los blancos estaban aposentándose en el vecino pueblo indígena de los sibundoyes, señores negligentes del amplio valle, del cual se dicen dueños, por un testamento de don Carlos, cacique de Santiago, en el que dispone de las tierras de Tamabioy, Tabancuan y Abuelapamba, colindantes con las de un capitán Ortiz, vecino de Aponte, las cuales fueron heredadas de sus abuelos, según dice al mismo testamento, de fecha 15 de marzo de 1700. Hablan los indios de otro testamento, otorgado por don Leandro Agreda, vecino de Sibundoy, el cual, y no el anterior, debe ser el pertinente; pero que no pudimos ver ni muestran a nadie, y agregan que el valle fue adquirido por el testador por compra hecha al rey de España por cuatrocientos patacones. Probablemente si la nación codiciara el valle como baldío, surgirán los legítimos títulos de propiedad." [Since long time ago, the whites had been settling in the neighboring indigenous town of the Sibundoyes, the gentlemen of the wide valley, of which they call themselves owners, because of a testament of Don Carlos, cacique of Santiago, in which he has the lands of Tamabioy, Tabancuan and Abuelapamba, adjacent to those of a captain Ortiz, neighbor of Aponte, which were inherited from their grandparents, according to the same testament, dated March 15, 1700.] Cfr. Miguel Triana, *Por el Sur de Colombia: Excursion Pintoresca y Científica al Putumayo* (Bogotá: Biblioteca Popular de Cultura Colombiana, 1907), 360. Juan Friede wrote that Bartolomé de Igualada, a priest that came to Sibundoy after the Capuchins had left, had a copy of Carlos Tamabioy's testament. Cfr. Juan Friede, "Leyendas de Nuestro Señor de Sibundoy y el Santo Carlos Tamabioy," *Boletín de Arqueología* 1, no. 4 (Julio–Agosto 1945): 317. In *Siervos de Dios y Amos de Indios: El Estado y la Misión Capuchina en el Amazonas*, Bonilla documents Tamabioy's testament. Cfr. Víctor Daniel Bonilla, *Siervos de Dios y Amos de indios: El estado y la Misión Capuchina en el Amazonas* (Bogotá: Stella, 1969).

    8. Alberto Juajibioy and Alvaro Wheeler indicate that the first meeting was in the month of July of 1535, not in June. Juajibioy and Wheeler, *Bosquejo Etnolingüístico del Grupo Kamsá de Sibundoy Putumayo, Colombia* (Bogotá: Instituto Lingüístico de Verano, 1973), 9. See also Bristol, "Sibundoy Ethnobotany," 18.

    9. Documento Communidad Camëntsá, *Procesos de Transformación y Alternativas de Autgestión Indígena* (Bogotá: Editorial ABC, 1989), 14. See also Gloria Stella Barrera Jurado, *Autonomía Artesanal: Creaciones y Resistencias del Pueblo Kamsá* (Bogotá: Pontificia Universidad Javeriana, 2015), 82.

    10. Bristol, "Sibundoy Ethnobotany," 19. See also Juajibioy and Wheeler, *Bosquejo Etnolingüístico*, 9. For a more detailed account of De Quesada's conquests, see: Juan Freide, *El Indio en Lucha por la Tierra: Historia de los Resguardos del Macizo Central Colombiano* (Bogotá: Ediciones La Chispa, 1944), 17–18.

    11. Michael Taussig, *Shamanism, Colonialism, and the Wild Man: A Study in Terror and Healing* (Chicago: University of Chicago Press, 1987). Taussing's view is also stated in the works of neo-granadinan historian Jose Antonio de Plaza. See Jose Antonio de Plaza, *Memorias para la Historia de la Nueva Granada* (Bogotá: Imprenta del Neogranadino, 1850), 126. The Pasto-Mocoa road, which crosses over the lands of Sibundoy, was officially inaugurated by the Capuchin mission in 1912, eight years after Sibundoy became the headquarters of the Apostolic Prefecture of Caquetá. This Apostolic Prefecture oversaw the territories of Caquetá, Putumayo, and the Colombian Amazon. Before 1912, Sibundoy was ecclesiastically affiliated with the Diocese of Pasto.

12. Juan Freide, "Archivo General de Indias—Sevilla. Patronato, legajo 189. Ramo 35," *Anuario Colombiano de Historia Social y de la Cultura* 4 (1969): 123.

13. Bonilla, *Siervos*, 24.

14. To be sure, the practice of agriculture implies that natives also knew that the well-being of the community depended on exploitation of the land. What became new to them was that land should be exploited more and more to satisfy people who did not even know how to work the land nor that human life could be conceived in terms of land alienation. As before indicated, the distinction between *Tsbatsanamamá* and *Fšants* reveals the material and the symbolic meaning of the land.

15. Citing well-known Colombian historian José María Alboreda Llorente, Haydée Seijas, says that in 1589, there were 700 tributary Indians. Seijas, "The Medical System of the Sibundoy Indians of Colombia" (PhD diss., Tulane University, 1969), 20. Bonilla indicates that in 1621, the *real* visitor don Luis de Quiñones reported 450 tributary Indians. Bonilla, *Siervos*, 25.

16. Marcelino de Castellví, "Historia Eclesiástica de la Amazonía Colombiana," *Revista Universidad Pontificia Bolivariana* 10, no. 36 (1944): 489. De Castellví also says that the Dominicans took over the Franciscans on March 23, 1577.

17. Seijas, "The Medical System," 79. Also: Bristol, "Sibundoy Ethnobotany," 26.

18. In other versions of the story, this working man did not see another person approaching. He saw a bird who was flying around him, as if inviting him to follow. And yet, in other versions, the man was working in what is today the west side of Sibundoy, on the way to Pasto: this detail implies that the icon of Christ had been carried to Pasto.

19. Kamëntšá men's traditional clothing.

20. This part is consistent in all versions of the story, suggesting that not all the natives of Sibundoy welcomed Christ, at least not initially.

21. While in some versions of the story, the offering of chicha is omitted, all stories indicate that natives had built a house for the Christ. Implicit in this part of the story is that there was acceptance of Christianity.

22. This part of the story, present in all versions of the story, seems to indicate that the icon of Christ was taken away from Sibundoy.

23. Historical references to this story are found in various documents. Omar Garzón Chivirí relates the story that Martín Agreda referred to him around 1998. Cfr. Omar Alberto Garzón Chivirí, *Rezar, Cantar, Soplar: Etnografía de una Lengua Ritual* (Quito, Ecuador: Ediciones Ayba-Yala, 2004), 26. Marcelino de Castellví makes reference to the "Christ of Sibundoy," which the Dominicans had taken from Sibundoy to Pasto when they took over the mission of Sibundoy, approximately in 1583. Cfr. De Castellví, "Historia Eclesiástica," 489.

24. Juan Freide, "Leyendas," 316.

25. Ibid., 317.

26. Seijas, "The Medical System," 74.

27. When he was writing about the history of the town of San Francisco, in 1952, Fray Jacinto Ma de Quito remembers that he had seen the deed of Carlos Tamabioy from Francisco Tisoy about forty years before. Jacinto Ma de Quito, *Historia de la Fundación del Pueblo de San Francisco en el Valle de Sibundoy* (Sibundoy: Edición Cicela, 1952), 23.

28. All the references to Carlos Tamabioy's testimony in this section come from Bonilla's book.

29. Bonilla, *Siervos*, 30.

30. De Quito, *Historia*, 24.

31. Bonilla, *Siervos*, 33.

32. Ibid., 35.

33. Ley Número 35 de 27-02-1888. "ARTICULO 31. Los convenios que se celebren entre la Santa Sede y el Gobierno de Colombia para el fomento de las misiones católicas en las tribus bárbaras no requieren ulterior aprobación del Congreso." [Law 35, February 27, 1888. Art 31. Covenants between the Holy See and the Colombian government concerning the fostering of Catholic missions among barbarous tribes do not require further approval by the [Colombian] Congress.] Cfr. Congreso de la República de Colombia, "Ley Número 35 de 27-02-1888," *Diario Oficial No. 7311* (1888).

34. In the appendix to his book, Bonilla presents the letters that Fray De Montclar wrote to his political friends, downplaying the complaints of the natives of Sibundoy as politically motivated. Bonilla, *Siervos*, 276–85.

35. Ibid.

36. De Quito, *Historia*, 5–6. Spanish version: "Este desacuerdo provenía de que los blancos habían tomado injustamente y aún de mala fe los terrenos de los indios, y éstos viéndose perjudicados en sus tierras, sementeras y casas, comenzaban a alejarse del pueblo y a vengarse de sus opresores siempre que podían."

37. Ibid., 7.

38. In Pasto City, the newspaper *Eco Liberal* started to publish complaints about the Capuchin missionaries because of the commercial activities with cattle by the missionaries, which contravened the commercial interests of the whites. Ibid., 18–19.

39. Ibid., 5. Original Spanish text: "Con pena advertía el antagonismo que había entre los niños de los blancos e indios, y casi siempre tenía quejas de unos y otros. Me convencía a menudo estar de parte de los indios la razón; pero los otros no reconocían su falte y en saliendo de la escuela se vengaban con insultos y puñetazos. A medida que me iba enterando de cómo vivían en el pueblo las dos razas, ví con mis propios ojos el odio que se tenían los unos con los otros. Persuadido entonces que esto no se podía remediar sino separándolos, me vino la idea de una fundación para los blancos en otra parte."

40. Law 41, 1904. According to this law, the whites of Sibundoy accepted the donation of native territories.

41. This is the Spanish version of the segment provided by De Quito: "Por este tiempo hubieron [*sic*] tres Caciques que entraron en razón y trabajaron con los Padres para que los demás accedieran a entregar los referidos terrenos. Se llamaban Miguel Guajivoy, Mariano Guajivoy y Alejo Jamioy." Cfr. De Quito, *Historia*, 24. Emphasis in the citation is mine.

42. The fragment from which the citation is taken, in Spanish, is as follows: "Al Sr. Padre Superior, han pedido un pedazo de terreno para los pobres blancos, y les damos el punto de Guaira-Sacha o San Francisco. Les damos voluntariamente para que edifiquen a los pobres blancos." Cfr. De Quito, *Historia*, 25.

43. Ibid., 26.

44. Simón Uribe, *Frontier Road: Power, History, and the Everyday State in the Colombian Amazon* (West Sussex, UK: John Wiley & Sons, 2017).

45. Ibid., 93.

46. Bonilla, *Siervos*, 84–86.

47. Uribe, *Frontier Road*, 95.

48. Ibid., 95.

49. Ibid.,109.

50. Ramón Vidal, "Critica histórica al libro de Victor D. Bonilla, 'Siervos de Dios y Amos de Indios,'" *Separata de Cultura Nariñense*, no. 25 (Julio 1970).

51. Ibid., 38.

52. Ibid., 54.

53. Ibid., 55. This is the Spanish version of the text that I translated into English: "[El transporte de blancos a espaldas de indios] era un servicio libre, organizado por los mismos indios y remunerado, y además el único medio posible de entrada al no existir camino alguno, como en el interior del país. Todos los blancos que entraban al territorio—incluso el general Rafael Reyes, futuro presidente, tuvieron que someterse a semejante servidumbre: pues era un auténtico sacrificio el viajar en tal forma."

54. Princeton Theological Seminary Library, "Las Misiones en Colombia: Obra de los Misioneros Capuchinos, de la Delegación Apostólica, del Gobierno y de la Junta Arquidiocesana Nacional en el Caquetá y Putumayo," Princeton Theological Seminary Library, https://archive.org/details/lasmisionesencol00unse (accessed July 2017). On page 23, one can read: "Para recorrer el trayecto entre la capital de Nariño y la residencia de los misioneros del Putumayo, empleaba una semana entera el viajero, llevado a espaldas de indio, que iba trepando con pies y manos por riscos espantables, al borde de vertiginosos abismos, y bajaba luego por precipicios como los que fingió Dante en el descenso al infierno. Hoy se salva aquella distancia en cuarenta y ocho horas, a caballo, por vía sólida y casi plana, sin peligro y sin cansancio."

55. Ibid., 24. Spanish version: "Entra el viajero al vallecito de Sibundoy, fértil y risueño como una añoranza del paraíso terrenal. Cinco años hace era región de salvajes y de fieras; álzanse hoy cinco risueños pueblecillos con su iglesia, y funcionan varias escuelas dirigidas por maestras alemanas, y que han presentado certámenes de gramática y aritmética, geografía e historia patrias, dignos de cualquier ciudad del interior."

56. Ibid., 25. "La cooperación a las misiones es trabajo en favor de la civilización universal, del progreso del humano linaje, y es obligación sagrada que nos impone el patriotismo; porque hay que hacer ciudadanos de los salvajes de hoy."

57. In the preface to his work, Bristol writes, "The town [Sibundoy], occupied almost entirely by white immigrants from the highlands of Nariño to the west, has about 275 households. . . . Monasteries and their associated schools occupied most of five of the towns' nineteen blocks." Cfr. Bristol, "Sibundoy Ethnobotany," iv. Later in the same work, he writes, "Both of the native cultural groups more than doubled their numbers during the years 1904–1940, but White immigration was so rapid that the European population, less than 10% of the total in 1904, climbed to 28% of the total in those 36 years, and by the 1960's had risen to around 60% of the valley's inhabitants." Cfr. Bristol, "Sibundoy Ethnobotany," 10. Seijas, on her part, wrote in 1965, "As in the rest of Colombia, the Indians of the Valley as a group are at the bottom of the social scale. This is made evident by the preference given to non-indians in all public places and accommodations such as school, church, and transportation; even in the cemeteries there is a section reserved for the non-Indians exclusively. Social intercourse between Indians and non-Indians is limited, mixed marriages are few and, with one exception, it is always the case of non-Indian males marrying Indian women." Cfr. Seijas, "The Medical System," 16.

58. As I will explain below, this is as true of Marcie Eliade's *Sacred and the Profane* and Ernst Cassirer's *Philosophy of Symbolic Forms*, Volume II.

59. See, for example, the works of N. Scott Momaday or Thomas King.

60. Wacknaité commemorates the spiritual presence of those who have died.

61. Baptism, first communion, and marriage required practicing this kind of speech. The generation of my parents used to exercise these speeches. In my generation, these kinds of speech are less frequent.

62. Juajibioy, *Lenguaje Ceremonial*, 25–30.

63. *Bëtaman jalesensian* used to be used in combination with *bëtaman jakorrintian*, but this older expression has been used with less frequency. Ibid.

64. Cfr. John H. McDowell, *So Wise Were Our Elders* (Lexington: University Press of Kentucky, 1994), 26. Some of the recordings of McDowell's trips are now stored at University of Texas, Austin's archive for languages in Latin America, now available online at: https://www.ailla.utexas.org/islandora/object/ailla%3A119513.

65. Garzón Chivirí, *Rezar*, 41–47. For a more detailed explanation on the ritual language in yajé ceremonies, see chapter 3 of the present work.

66. McDowell, *Sayings of the Ancestors: The Spiritual Life of the Sibundoy Indians* (Lexington: University Press of Kentucky, 1989), vii.

67. Ibid., 2. Among others, McDowell follows Tzvetan Todorov's view that Amerindian societies have mastered the "art of ritual discourse," to indicate that "the central elements in the Sibundoy folk religion . . . are surely cornerstones of Amerindian consciousness." Ibid., 5–6.

68. Ibid., 2.

69. Ibid., 2.

70. Ibid., 2.

71. In the Inga dictionary, *Ñugpamanda* is characterized as an adjective that denotes ancestry, not necessarily primacy. Cfr. Stephen H. Levinsohn, *The Inga Language* (The Hague, Netherlands: Mouton & Co B.V. Publishers, 1976), 114.

72. Francisco Tandioy Jansasoy and Stephen H. Levinsohn, *Diccionario Inga* (Santiago, Putumayo: Comité de Educación Inga de la Organización Musu Runakuna, 1997), 73.

73. McDowell, *Sayings*, 24.

74. Ibid., 24. Given the historical context of the Sibundoy Valley and the syncretic religious elements that have been incorporated into the native cultures after the conquest, it is difficult to

assert that an earlier founding spirituality had remained intact over the years. As I will explain in chapter 3, Catholic iconography gets along with native religious ceremonies of healing.

75. Ibid., 25.
76. Ibid., 4.
77. Ibid., 7.
78. Ibid.,162.
79. Ibid., 164.
80. Ibid., 23.
81. Justo Jacanamijoy España, Juan Bautista Jacanamijoy Juajibioy, and Carlos Jamioy Narváez, *Camëntša Cabëngbe Ntšayanana* (Sibundoy: Uámana Soyënga Camëntšañe Uatsjéndayënga, 1994), 1.
82. McDowell, *Sayings*, 46.
83. Ibid., 3.
84. Ibid., 47.
85. Ibid., 104.
86. Ibid., 106.
87. In his second book, *So Wise Were Our Elders*, he recognizes that he borrowed these terms from Levi-Strauss. He writes: "As Roberta Segal . . . correctly notes, Lévi-Strauss singled out the mastery of fire as the key step in a transition from an animal-like state of nature to a distinctively human state of culture. The chief symbol of that transition was the shift described in North and especially South American Indian myths from eating food raw to eating it cooked. Taita Bautista's invocation of the raw time as a counter to the way things are done today captures the prominence of this same emphasis on the symbolic importance of fire in the Kamsá account of the emergence of civilization." Cfr. McDowell, *So Wise*, 40.
88. The story has been published in Kamëntšá language since 1973. Cfr. Juajibioy and Wheeler, *Bosquejo Etnolingüístico*, 28. Here is the story in Kamëntšá where "Wangëtsmen" is mentioned only once:

> Inye tempo Kabá tonday iñe yendmëña ora, yentxanga nye kakana mnasáy. Kanye tena mnenëngmëmnay iñama ora, alwaserofja yejabbokna jauyanama: "Atx xkoblegá iñe jwaboknama, pero nyetskanga bolleto xmochtatxetáy, i ndoñe chká kexmonjaxbwachenasná, ndoñe pabor kbwatjabiama". Yentxanga mojenoyeunaisna, mojaxbwachena bolleto jatxetayama. Chora alwaserofjna yejochumo wangëtsmenbioy, nye chá iñe bomná inamna.
> Chabentxe yejamashngo orna bojauyana: "¿Taitá kbebiajwá?" Bojojwá: "aber xmebiajwá". Chora yejóntxa jalantsan washwatxujwá yejtsasjojnaise. Ndeolpna yeñoy yejóbekoná i waskwatxujwakacheban iñe yejaftsabajkesna. Betsko shjoye yejisatatxena i tjañe yejaujkushashe. Kachora yejwangbototjo nsachetxá yejojkushasbiñe. Chora yentxanga mojabokana iñe jokñama.
> Chorskana iñe katnjanobinyna kem lwar. I shienná mats yojandelejensia jwashntsama. Chentxán xbwachán katnjanonymá kem Iwar."

89. Ibid., 9–18.
90. Ibid., 2.
91. Ibid., 14.
92. Ibid., 15.
93. Ibid., 15
94. Stith Thompson, *Tales of the North American Indians*, 1969. Cited by McDowell, *So Wise*, 15.
95. Ibid., 16.
96. John H. McDowell, "Exemplary Ancestors and Pernicious Spirits: Sibundoy Concepts of Cultural Evolution," in *Traditional Storytelling Today: An International Sourcebook*, ed. Margaret Read MacDonald (Chicago: Fitzroy Dearborn Publishers, 1999), 513–21.
97. In addition to Mircea Eliade whom I here discuss, philosopher Ernst Cassirer, early in his career, believed that human consciousness takes on different modes and expresses its modes of thinking through symbols, which together form human culture. In Cassirer's mind, culture is

the synthesis of all symbolic forms. Influenced by Kant, Cassirer argued in the second volume of *Symbolic Forms* that mythology plays an ancillary function in the development of consciousness, and that scientific modes of thinking play a more crucial role in the civilizing process of the human mind. Mythic thinking, he believed, is the most prominent feature of primitive consciousness, while analytic thinking is more prominent of civilized consciousness. Like Eliade, Cassirer believed that primitive societies did not have the creative elements to rise above themselves through categorical forms of human understanding. Cfr. Ernst Cassirer, *Mythical Thought*, vol. 2 of *The Philosophy of the Symbolic Forms* (New Haven, CT: Yale University Press, 1955), 59. Later in his life, Cassirer qualified his view of mythic thinking. In *An Essay on Man*, he wrote that myth is not a system of dogmatic creeds. "It consists much more in actions than in mere images or representations," he declared, adding, "Even if we should succeed in analyzing myth into ultimate conceptual elements, we could, by such an analytic process, never grasp its vital principle, which is a dynamic not a static one; it is describable only in terms of action. . . . Primitive man expresses his feelings and emotions not in mere abstract symbols but in a concrete and immediate way; and we must study the whole of this expression in order to become aware of the structure of myth and primitive religion." Cfr. Ernst Cassirer, *An Essay on Man* (New Haven, CT: Yale University Press, 1967), 79.

98. Mircea Eliade, *Myth and Reality*, trans. Willard R. Trask (Long Grove, IL: Harper & Row, 1963), 6.

99. Eliade, *Myth of the Eternal Return*, trans. Willard R. Trask (Princeton, NJ: Princeton University Press, 1954), 4–5.

100. Ibid.

101. Thomas M. Alexander, *The Human Eros: Eco-Ontology and the Aesthetics of Existence* (New York: Fordham University Press, 2013).

102. Ibid., 403.

103. Ibid., 405.

104. Ibid., 412.

105. I primarily follow the works of N. Scott Momaday, Leslie Silko, and Thomas King. For a more detailed reflection on the meaning and practices of storytelling, see Margaret Read McDonald (ed.), *Traditional Storytelling Today: An International Sourcebook* (New York: Routledge, 1999).

106. N. Scott Momaday, *The Man Made of Words* (New York: St Martin's Griffin, 1997), 28–29.

107. Ibid., 15.

108. Ibid., 55.

109. Thomas King, *The Truth about Stories: A Native Narrative*, 1st ed. (Minneapolis: University of Minnesota Press, 2008), 9.

110. Seijas wrote that "in 1966 approximately 40 percent of the Sibundoy Indian population between 15 and 59 years of age, inclusive, was engaged in cuadrillas." And she added, "Because of the increasing cost of food, the demands in time and energy for the preparation of meals and chicha for the workers, and their growing needs for cash income, those Indian who have a sizable crop surplus prefer to sell it and hire peons rather than to depend on *cuadrillas* or the more expensive mingas." Cfr. Seijas, "The Medical System," 97.

Chapter Two

Beauty in Kamëntšá Culture

Nothing binds Kamëntšá and Inga peoples more deeply with each other and with the rest of Mother Nature (that is, the significant place of origin) than a celebration of what they deem the most important day of the year: the day of the dancing of forgiveness—"Atún Puncha" in the Inga language and "Bëtšknaté" in Kamëntšá. As a Kamëntšá myself, I dance to maintain the deep connection with all the people, for my memory echoes the wisdom of my elders who understood the arrival of the beautiful dance that initiated a new form of collective consciousness. Despite its cultural transformation over the years, this dancing is a constituting symbol of the Kamëntšá culture, one that takes up the fundamental forces of life itself. But it is also a constituted symbol, one that has a history and enacts a ritual of forgiveness. After describing the cultural transformation of the dancing in this chapter, I argue that Kamëntšás' dancing of forgiveness is an aesthetic celebration of existence as it fundamentally appears to Kamëntšás, with suffering and joyfulness, with restraint and freedom, with actuality and possibility, with past and present. I intend to demonstrate that in celebrating these recurring dichotomies of human existence, in taking together an enactment of the past in the present, the dancing is also a symbol of human existence. As the general purpose of my work is to articulate the most general symbolic manifestations of the Kamëntšá culture in terms of its constituted and constituting symbols, in this chapter I demonstrate that Bëtšknaté, like storytelling, provides an aesthetically constituted and constituting meaning to human life.

Scholarship concerning Bëtšknaté is very limited. A few Sibundoy visitors have barely mentioned it, some associating it with the Corpus Christi celebration and others with agricultural festivities. Describing the methods of consuming maize in Sibundoy, in 1965, Bristol described the Bëtšknaté as the Christian Mardi Gras superimposed on the old Sibundoy New Year festivities, which take place in late February or early March. He also wrote that the main activities are "playing flutes and drums, getting dressed up, and getting drunk," and that on his stay in Sibundoy he saw his neighboring native family organize a party for several days and prepare more than a hundred gallons of chicha, which they and their guests consumed in three days.[1] Omar Garzón Chivirrí describes the Bĕtšknaté as a feast of forgiveness that marks the new year for the natives of Sibundoy. "This is the time," he says, "to prepare the land to plant maize, but it is also the time of reconciliation and of conjuring the colonial forces that came to the town with the arrival of the Spaniards and stretched more significantly with the Capuchin mission."[2]

Scholarship on indigenous dancing and indigenous aesthetics has so much emphasized the religious aspect that it has not allowed any room to interpret dancing as creative and transformative aesthetically. Speaking of the anthropological challenge of using one's concepts to describe the experiences of others, Stanley Jeyaraja Tambiah has correctly pointed out that anthropologists must be careful when they describe the experiences of other cultures as religious. "Religion," he said, "in English is normally associated with the idea of a supernatural, of a transcendental power to which humans have relations of obligation and piety."[3] Tambiah's warning is pertinent here, as one of the traditional ways of interpreting native dancing is mainly in terms of religion. Scholars on native South American culture, for example, often cite the writings of Rafael Krasten, who, in 1926, suggested that native aesthetics must be interpreted in terms of their religious significance. He wrote that customs related to self-decorating have not, in the first place, been practiced merely for decorative or embellishing purposes but that they have emerged from religious ideas.[4] While the Bĕtšknaté has some syncretic religious symbolism, its significance rests on the fact that we as natives engaged in an aesthetic celebration of life.

In understanding native dancing as merely a religious manifestation, the creative element of the natives and the process of transformation during the dancing becomes secondary. It is true that the Bĕtšknaté has a ritualistic element, especially the element of forgiveness, which could be interpreted as a religious manifestation of the culture, but most of the spontaneous expressions should better be understood as driven by the need for aesthetic experiences, not as ways to approach the divine. One can recognize the religious elements belonging to the dancing but should not disregard the fact that the dancing is mainly an aesthetic celebration.

In the Kamĕntšá language, there is a distinction between *fšants* and *Tsbatsanamamá*. *Fšants* is the piece of land used for the basic needs, mainly for nourishment. *Tsbatsanamamá* (or *Tsabatsan-mamá*) is Land at large, or what we call "Mother Earth," and she is the unifying force of all existing things.[5] As explained before, the distinction between these two denominations is to emphasize the symbolic meaning of the universe, created through time, and functioning as the basis for answering to the quest for meaning in Time. In dancing, we celebrate our having *fšants*, which give us physical fortitude, and the binding force that unifies us deeply, our mother Earth, or *Tsbatsanamamá*. We thus dance as members of a big family, immediately manifested in the presence of others, but symbolically manifested in the awareness that we share existence with other creatures of the universe. To treat dancing as "religious" then suggests a separation between the people and Nature: Nature is seen as something that is worshipped rather than as one's family in which one participates.

Bětsknaté is a celebration of being, as it fundamentally appears to Kamëntšás. Through generations, the members of this culture have noticed that all existing things come to be, flourish, and eventually die. Human condition, they claim, follows a similar path. "We are today here, dancing, but we might not be able to dance next year," express the dancers. And, while dancing, they continue, saying, "Our ancestors danced here, in our land, their positive and negative energies remain with us, but not all of them can sing with us, and there might come a day when one of us might not be remembered." Instead of taking a pessimistic stance to life, the dancers celebrate life as it comes; we assume that there is no other option other than to celebrate existence as it comes, with pain, suffering, hope, and tragedy.

The significance of Bětsknaté comes from the fact that this is a celebration of the experience of beauty. I would like to develop this claim in the following three sections. In the first section, I present one of the foundational stories of Bětsknaté, and I comment on three of its important aspects: first, the distinction between land as a physical space and land as a symbolic conception of nature; second, the primacy of the community over the individual; and third, the drinking of chicha. In the second section, I present another story that gives continuity to the former and explains the ritual of forgiveness as it is at present practiced in the dancing. In the third section, I present the characters of the dancing, giving especial emphasis to the *Sanjuanëng*, the characters that embody suffering in all its forms. Finally, and to give continuity to the general argument of this work, in the last section, I conclude by showing why the Bětsknaté should be considered aesthetically, as the embodiment of a philosophy of life.

I. BĚTSKNATÉ AS CONSTITUTED SYMBOL: ORIGINS AND CULTURAL TRANSFORMATIONS

Kamëntšá elders narrate linearly neither the origins of Bětskanté nor its different denominations or ritual origins. Depending on the elements that they want to emphasize, they could start from the cultural transformation of the past century when the Capuchin mission arrived in Sibundoy or from a different epoch. What is clear, however, is that the oldest is the story that gives the dancing a proper name, the Bëtsknaté. Then comes the story that narrates the origin of the ritual of forgiveness and changes the name from "Bëtsknaté" to "Clestrinÿe." As I will describe in the third section of this chapter, the third narrative account comes from the time when the Catholic Church and the Spanish colonization modified the dancing. In chronologically describing the dancing and its cultural transformations, I want to indicate that despite its cultural transformation, a form of celebrating and understanding life as it fundamentally appears underlies this practice of dancing. In my interpretation, I do not deny the importance of clothes and all the artistic elements that shape the dancing, but I want to emphasize that the main significance of the dancing does not come from its cultural transformation but from the recurring aesthetic symbols used to represent existence. In as much as one can agree that those fundamental characters of human existence are transculturally experienced, one can say that this dancing is a living symbol of human life.

The oldest of the stories of our dancing speaks of a time when people merely worked, void of celebration and deprived of a sense of unity. Food and land were abundant, but the arts did not exist. There were only stories. Slowly, there emerged a time when birds started to sing earlier in the morning, their voices enticing *Šinÿe* (Father Sun) to wake up earlier and to shine more pleasantly. As no father can resist the claims of his children, the Sun could not resist the melodies of the birds and began to rise earlier. *Tsbatsanamamá* (Mother Earth) thus gave birth to colorful flowers, exciting the sensibilities of the elders. However, they increased their labor, became busier, while their minds focused on toiling their land, sensing the pressure of uneasiness and incompleteness of existence. Then, one day, the sound of the birds resembled sounds of harmonicas, flutes, and drums. Confused, the elders stopped working and turned around, their clothes still dirty. On the horizon of the east was a group of beautiful people, dressed in beautiful colors, their belts as perfectly crafted as their music.[6] Now in circles, now in lines, they came dancing, singing, and inviting everyone to join, saying, "*Tšams Kabunga, tšams bundatë, vida ora, joboijuam*" meaning, "Because we are the same, because we are together, while alive we must dance." All joined the dancers, learned the music, and became intoxicated with chicha, corn-made beer. When sobriety returned, nobody knew from where the visitors had come, nor where they went. They only knew that it was the greatest of days, worthy of a proper name, *Bëtsknaté* in Kamëntšá language.

Several elements of this oldest story deserve comment. The story of Bëtsknaté indicates that the valley looked gloomy before the dancing, its scattered families toiling the land with no higher purpose other than to supply their basic needs, all fearful of wild spirits of the shadows, which the faint sun rays could not destroy. It was a time when they had a sense of *fšants* but not a more refined understanding of *Tsbatsanamamá*. As before indicated, when the elders speak of the land as the source of food and nutrition, they refer to it as *fšants*; when they want to convey a deeper meaning, they refer to the land as *Tsbatsanamamá*.[7] In the story, one can see that there is a sense of incompleteness in the idea of constantly working the land to be successful. While at present this sense of incompleteness associated with working the land constantly has lost its original meaning, there is a general agreement that people not participating in the dancing are somehow empty.[8]

One can also see in this oldest story the primacy of the community—rather than the individual—in the dancing. It is a dancing of unification that has marked a new conscious mode of being, a way of being beautifully alive with the rest of nature and other family members, a sense of unity that one can still feel in today's dancing. While this old story of Bëtšknaté is powerful, its significance lies in the fact that it exhorts us to dance, to take a moment of life and enjoy it as it comes. Early in my life, I learned that in Bëtšknaté we celebrate the arrival of Beauty—which is the dance itself—to the village and the brotherhood that she has established. With her charms, songs, and clothes, Beauty came to create the bonds of brotherhood and established a new sense of meaningfulness—a sense of communal participation with all existing things. But the story also says that Beauty did not stay in the village. At present, she comes and goes, in cycles, like life itself. When she left, the ancestors went back to toiling the land, now with more energy and the hope of celebrating her return. It is part of the wisdom of the ancestors that each time we are dancing we are celebrating what we learned from her, honoring her arrival with our music and our crafts.

Finally, this foundational story narrates not only the beginning of the dancing ceremony but also the intoxication through maize-beer, *Bëkoy* in Kamëntšá language. *Bëkoy* is consumed routinely for nourishment, refreshment, and enjoyment[9] ; for the dancing, it must be more fermented and prepared in abundance. As drinking *Bëkoy* is fundamental for the dancing, it deserves some comment here.

There is a story of the woman *Bëkoy*, whom McDowell interprets as a symbol of divine punishment. The story is about a beautiful woman who wanted to marry a young man and went to live with his family before marriage. The future mother-in-law did not like her, and in the absence of the fiancé, she forced the bride to do all the chores of the house, including work at the *jajañ* (native garden) and preparing three earthen pots of chicha with three bushels. The young woman, says the story, managed to prepare chicha with only one grain of corn. When the would-be mother-in-law returned, the young woman was sitting on the porch, combing her hair, the three bushels of corn intact by her side, except for the one that had a grain taken away. On seeing this, the old woman scolded the bride, and she, crying angrily, protested that she had done her job. Then, warning that in the future there would not be anyone else who knows how to make chicha with one single grain of corn, the bride became a bird, plunged into the chicha, spilled it all over the house, and flew away. Slowly, the ants came to drink it.

On McDowell's view, this story accounts for the "harsh realities of the human condition,"[10] suggesting that hard labor among the Sibundoy natives is the result of divine punishment. The gods, says McDowell, had sent the young woman to "teach women how to make chicha with relatively little effort."[11] But the bride, he adds, "taking umbrage at the undeserved rough treatment she receives from the older woman . . . decides not to convey the vital piece of information but instead transforms into a shulupsi bird."[12] The explanation of why men and women must labor so hard to find a living in this world rests on this story[13]; for, "it was meant to be otherwise," continues McDowell, "but as a consequence of human frailty displayed by the mother-in-law, extensive plots of corn must be planted, weeded, trimmed, and harvested and large piles of grain must be ground and cooked, for people to survive."[14]

McDowell is partly justified to provide such an interpretation, since he visited the generation of whole-hearted Catholic natives who faced harsh conditions of land exploitation by white settlers at the beginning of the last century and who yet found consolation in the Catholic teachings that God prefers the poor. By the 1960s, all natives of Sibundoy had learned that the survival of the community depended on stoically enduring the forces of colonialism and accepting the hard laboring conditions.

The story of the chicha woman takes on those historical challenges of cultural transformation. It is not fortuitous that dreaming of chicha still today is associated with expecting heavy rainy days, which metaphorically symbolizes expecting unfavorable days for crops. In McDowell's collection of sayings, the Ingas say, "*Asua muscugpica, tamia puncha tugungapa*";[15] in the Kamëntšá culture, we say, "*Bocoy tcojotjená, ana bëtsaye juaftenä.*"[16] Both expressions mean, "If you dream chicha, it will rain heavily."

I remember that the story of the chicha woman came up in the context of a conversation on the differences between the generations of my grandparents and my parents in the days before Bëtšknaté. My mom told me the story for the first time when I was ten, and I asked her how she had learned to make chicha and why my grandmother on my father's side often said that warmed-up chicha tastes like the real chicha of Bëtšknaté. My mom explained to me that before traders and missionaries introduced grinding mills to Sibundoy, the making of chicha required the use of grinding stones. When they learned of the grinding mills, some of the elders refused to drink the chicha that came from them. It did not taste as good as the old way of making it. On my interpretive horizon, to use Gadamer's expression, the young woman represents a new generation that makes chicha using grinding mills, thus challenging the older generation. As I understood my mom, in creating a story of this cultural transformation, the elders slowly condensed the challenges of adopting cultural elements into their culture.

II. FROM BËTŠKNATÉ TO CLESTRINŸË

The second story of Bëtšknaté, which gives continuity to the former story, speaks of the origin of the ritual of forgiveness that is still alive in today's dancing. This second story describes the time when the elders were unsure of the right time to dance again. Hopeful, they waited for Mother Nature to give them some signs. One day some elders saw beautiful violet flowers growing, which later became to be known as *Clestrinÿë* and were at the time interpreted as signs of Mother Earth's call for dancing. As they took those flowers, some remembered how to dance and others not. Those who did not remember started to feel a growing sense of alienation in their hearts, their faces turning as gray as the clouds before raining. Fearful that they might not be able to dance again, they asked for help. Those who did remember the dance decided to throw petals on the heads of those forgetful so as to help remind them how to dress up, dance, and sing. Eventually everyone remembered how to dance and make crafts and music. Because dancing came back, it brought about a ritual and became known as *Clestrinÿë*.

Unlike the oldest story, which emphasizes the origins of dancing itself, the newer story speaks of the origins of forgiveness. This cultural shift is important to explore both because of its philosophical significance and because it tells of a cultural change when Bëtšknaté was denominated to Clestrinÿë. Kamëntšá language uses suffixes to qualify nouns. The word Clestrinÿë contains the morpheme *inÿë*, used to indicate awakening, illumination, clarity, and balance. *Inÿë* is present in words like *bominÿë* (eyes), *Šinÿë* (sun), *ninÿë* (firewood), and *binÿë* (wind), all of which carry a semantic meaning that emphasizes clarity, awakening, and illumination. The word *binÿë* carries a deeper metaphysical significance to the Kamëntšá culture, for the expression *binÿë wasjanjaná* (literally, whipped by a bad wind) means that a person is ill because of an imbalance of his or her energies with the rest of nature.[17] This brief linguistic explanation helps us see why some elders decided to equate Bëtšknaté with Clestrinÿë. In naming it Clestrinÿë, the dance became a symbol of light for the native collective consciousness, a way of representing the human need to remain in balance and harmony with the rest of nature. As I will explain in the next section of this chapter, death is an extreme form of forgetfulness. When nobody remembers one's existence any longer, one is gone; one is taken by the infinite ocean of complete forgetfulness. Flowers here symbolize the fragility of human memory, their growing and dying a reminder of our powers to remember and forget. The throwing of Clestrinÿë petals onto the heads of those who suffer from weak memory becomes a symbol of the human condition of forgetfulness. With the throwing of flowers onto someone else's head, the Kamëntšá culture celebrates memory and forgetfulness. In today's celebration, we still have this ritual of throwing petals on someone else's head, despite that now, because of Catholic teachings, it is mainly seen as a ritual of forgiveness.

Whether one emphasizes the story of the beginning of dancing and wants to call it Bëtšknaté or whether one takes the awakening of harmony among the members of this native community through the throwing of flowers to be the most significant ritual and wants to call it Clestrinÿë, the dancing stands out as the mark of a new kind of consciousness among the Kamëntšás. In the most general terms, it continues to be the symbolic, aesthetic enactment of what it means to live as human, living through suffering and joyfulness, with forgetfulness and memory. The arrival of the Capuchin mission at the beginning of the last century changed significantly the material components of the dancing, specifically with the introduction of the ritual of the beheading of an old rooster and the refinement of the *Sanjuanëng* characters. Their arrival nonetheless did not change the underlying philosophy of the dancing. Despite its external changes, one can still see that the spirit of the dancing and its symbolic meaning are alive. Before detailing its philosophical significance, the dancing must be explained in its newest form, as it is performed today.[18]

III. BËTŠKNATÉ AS A CONSTITUTING SYMBOL: AN EXPERIENCE OF DANCING

If one asked any contemporary Kamëntšá about Bëtšknaté, they would probably tell how the dancing is performed each year. Using Kamëntšá and Spanish language with pride, the Kamëntšás of today say that Bëtšknaté starts and ends at the heart of each family, where all hearts must be in harmony. On *Waishanyá*, a local Kamëntšá radio station, days before Bëtšknaté, one can hear:

> Bëtšknaté, bëngbiam botaman y puert wachwanté endmën. . . . Cheté montšantenebj nÿetska pamilliang . . . korent oyejuyká mochantsebersiá. . . . Chtén kach yebnokan mochanjabojatšá, chëntšán bëtsna choy kochajenobokn, chëntš inÿe pamilingabtkang mochajeninšen, y chor kokayé, bëngbe tabanoy mochajanašekuast, nÿetskan oyejuaiká. . . . Tabanok echansatobatmán bëngbe Taitamandad, Arkanÿe, Alguacer, y Watekmëng . . . chentšan mochanjenatsekuatš Arkaÿbioy joboyejuam . . . inÿe pamilianbioknak mochanjabsatsëtsay . . . chté, bokoy, saná, oyejuaiká, kochatenanjá. [The Bëtšknaté is for us a beautiful and powerfully reconnecting day. . . . On that day we will reconnect with all our families . . . and we will sing happily. . . . On that day we will start from our homes and then we should gather at in the

center of Sibundoy with other families and then, of course! To the heart of Sibundoy, we will go, everyone celebrating. . . . At the heart of Sibundoy, our political leaders will be waiting for us . . . and from there we should go to visit and dance into their houses and into other families' houses. . . . On that day, we will share with everyone food and chicha happily.]

Each Kamëntšá family initiates the dancing at home, asking neighbors to join the dance with the same melody their ancestors used, singing, "Tšams kabënga / tsams bundata; / vida ora joboyjuama; / ndas koktsemn, moibuambás; / vida ora / joboyjuama / chok, chok, chok / mok, mok, mok . . . hihihi! [We are the same / we are together; / if we are alive / we should dance; / haven't met you yet? / Sing along; / if there is life / we should dance / there, there, there / here, here, here . . . hihihi!]" They all go to the heart of Sibundoy's boroughs where the first collective meeting initiates. With the help of horns, drums, flutes, and harmonicas, all adults sing and dance. Children play at pleasure. At the meeting, there is one main character who presides over the dancing, and he or she is followed by four different groups. The rest of the community dances after the four groups. Except for the *Sanjuanëng* group who walks, all participants dance on the way to the cathedral, the mayor's office, and to the most sacred of Kamëntšás' homes, the *Waman Posadok* (the most sacred house). The dancing does not conclude in *waman posadok*. After visiting the sacred place, one can join a group and go to different houses, always dancing.

The first and perhaps most respected of the characters is the *Mëtëtsen* (Matachín), the symbol of Father Sun. Wearing a red mask, the Matachín walks dancing, calling, with the sounds of a bell, everyone to join the dance, his neck covered with colorful beads entwined with long sharp teeth and his head crowned with feathers. His walking alone means that the oldest of the people who brought the dancing to the village is gone. As he represents Father Sun, his calling is a symbol of guidance and illumination.

Next is the *Yentsayauabinyanayëng* (men carrying flags), a group of twelve people chosen by the leaders of the community to represent Jesus's twelve disciples. Carrying flags of different colors, these men dance in circles, and when they stop, they greet each other with the flags, making crosses. Current and past political leaders of the community, all dancing, follow the *Yentsayauabinyanayëng*.

Third in the dancing go the *Sarawayengä*, a small group of four to ten men who represent white colonizers. With trapezoid-like crowns, covered with mirrors and cotton, they dance slowly, as if they don't know how to dance.[19] But they look proud, wearing white pants and white T-shirts, a red tunic bundled at their necks and hanging on their backs. Their mirrors symbolize the deceitful ways that the conquistadors used to rob and exploit the land. It is believed that these personages were introduced in the late 1970s, to commemorate the Corpus Christi festivity. They also represent the missionaries who would give Kamëntšás European clothes, candies, and other trifles to convince them of the truth of baptism.

The *Sarawayengä* are immediately followed by the *Sanjuanëng*, who represent all forms of destruction and all the causes of suffering. The most complex of the symbols in the dancing and the most controversial of the figures, the *Sanjuanëng* symbolically are the embodiment of all kinds of suffering, including its most radical forms, destruction and death.

In the Kamëntšá culture, we distinguish two types of sufferings: the unqualified and the qualified. Unqualified suffering, or *ngmenan*, does not depend entirely on human intervention; it comes from the cycle of life itself. The unexpected death of a loved one, child, youth, or adult is always *ngmenan*. It is painful, but it is also part of the cycle of life. The forgetfulness of our roots, our own limitation is also *ngmenan*; to forget someone or something is to bury him, her, or the event, and it is also *ngmenan*. The qualified type of suffering is the one that depends on human action, and it has different denominations, depending on the actions and intentions of the agent. The worst type of person is the one who is resourceful and finds the means to cause harm to others. We call that person *bakawamaná* or *podeskwamaná*; this character is the worst because her or his sacred part, *waman*, is compromised in the act; the *bakawamaná* acts alone, willingly, intelligently, and without hiding him- or herself in the act. Still very bad, but not as bad as *bakawamaná*, is the *opá* or the *buakwaná*; these characters cause harm but not in an intelligent manner. The *opá* normally needs the help of another person to cause harm, and the *buakwaná* causes harm in secret, pretending otherwise to be a good person. There is more hope in improving the character of the *opá* and *buakwaná*, as these characters are not using their sacred part to cause harm. There is also a type of suffering that comes from thinking bad of another person. Thinking bad of another person without doing anything else belongs to the unqualified type of suffering; it is *ngeman* because it is possible to think bad of another without intention. The *Sanjuanëng* embody these forms of sufferings and bad moral characters.

Regarding their appearance, the dismayed faces of the *Sanjuanëng* bear a mounting infirmity of the ancestors' past. When nobody remembers anything of his or her existence or of the existence of the Kamëntšá community, we, the Kamëntšás, will be all dead. As they aim to represent the powers of destruction, the *Sanjuanëng* are the only group of people who do not dance. Wearing dirty pants and boots and covering their heads with ugly, almost formless black masks, they walk mournfully, with the help of a stick. On the top of their masks, they carry skins of animals, and on their backs big baskets. They are present in the dancing not only because of the suffering caused by the European conquest, but also because they represent the sanctions of bad behavior within the community, like stealing, forgetfulness, and harming others. As previously indicated, for the Kamëntšás, death is an extreme form of forgetfulness. Presumably these characters were introduced prior to the arrival of the Spanish conquistadors, but they become more complex with the arrival of the Spaniards to the region.

In today's symbolism, one can see that the *Sanjuanëng* have refined their representation of suffering. This is true from the fact that when the dancing is about to conclude formally, just in front of *Waman Posadok* (the most sacred of Kamëntšá's houses), the *Sanjuanëng* are responsible for beheading an old rooster. A combination of symbols allows us to see that the sacrifice of an old rooster is not only a representation of the extreme cruelty that came to the imagination of Kamëntšás with the arrival of the European conquest but also the way Kamëntšás understood the teachings of missionaries. Some elders have told me that this is the representation of how natives were destroyed by the conquistadors. Others indicated to me that the *Sanjuanëng* are the representation of those Kamëntšás who committed suicide when they were oppressed. Despite this difference of opinions, there is agreement that the *Sanjuanëng* are the symbol of pain, death, and destruction.

A group of elderly women dancing around the image of the Virgin Mary follows the *Sanjuanëng* on their way to the cathedral. When asked for the meaning of their dancing around the Virgin Mary, some of the elderly women say that it reminds them of the times when Kamëntšá people used to travel long distances to exchange some of the local products of Mother Earth. It is worth noting how the Virgin Mary took on the notion of *Tsbatsanamamá*, suggesting a syncretic form of symbolism. The dancing of the elderly women together concludes formally at the cathedral in Sibundoy, but their individual participation continues.

Following these first groups, the rest of the community dances, each member dressed as beautifully as possible. Parents tell children that only in Bëtšknaté must they be concerned about dressing beautifully. Normally all adults save their best clothes for this occasion. Inspired by the beautiful landscapes of the region, artists create belts, handicrafts, necklaces, and crowns; some prefer to see the colors that the ancestors saw and prepare to participate in rituals of healing and purification, but this is not expected or required. One can infer the aesthetic meaning of this celebration from the mastery, dedication, and skills of Kamëntšá artists in making the most beautiful clothes for Bëtšknaté. At no other time can one see Kamëntšás caring more about happiness and enjoyment. Elders usually wear a big crown with sixteen belts hanging around the rim and save their best clothes for this celebration. Proud and elegant, they chant and dance with the young and the children.

In addition to the ritual of beheading an old rooster, which takes place at the end of the formal celebration, there is the celebration of forgiveness, which takes place in the central plaza. At once a public and a private event, the ritual of forgiveness consists in throwing petals of Clestrinÿë flowers on one another while asking for forgiveness. It is assumed that no one is so perfect not to ask or deny forgiveness to another. Even if one has not offended anyone, it is hard to imagine that one does not think bad of another person. As the story above described indicated, there was a time when some elders could not remember when the right time to dance was. The story says that with the act of throwing petals of the flowers, they soon remembered not only how to dance but also how to sing and make crafts. With the arrival of the Catholic Church, the act of throwing flowers acquired a new meaning. It came to signify that there cannot be a true enjoyment of the music when there is disharmony. Some Kamëntšá elders even say that they decided to restore harmony among themselves from the differences that they had with respect to the value of the Catholic teachings. Apparently, an internal division was created after the arrival of the Capuchin mission, as some were more willing to follow the teachings than others. These differences did not, however, destroy the spirit of the dancing, for the spirit of the dancing has always been to reconcile the most difficult of human existence's dichotomies. Despite differences, fundamental to the Kamëntšá culture is the view that we all are ultimately brothers and sisters, all children of Mother Nature. The initial ritual of throwing petals to remember how to dance is now a ritual of forgiveness, of the idea that despite our differences we need to reconcile with others if we want to dance collectively, that is, if we don't want to alienate ourselves from the rest of nature.

Although Kamëntšás had heard of the Catholic Church since 1577 when the Dominican Order stayed at the village for six years, it was only in the last century that Catholic teachings and the Spanish heritage permeated the community more strongly. At the beginning of the last century, the Colombian State entrusted the Capuchin Order with the mission of civilizing all natives of the south of Colombia. The Capuchins and then other missionaries forced the leaders to agree on allowing the natives of Sibundoy to celebrate the Bëtšknaté on the Sunday before Ash Wednesday and to include in the dancing a procession of the symbol of Mother Mary from the outskirts of the town to the cathedral where a regional bishop would give a Mass. Despite this cultural transformation, one can see that the deep philosophical meaning of the dancing was not transformed with the arrival of Catholicism. It is clear from observing that the Kamëntšás have used their creative powers to respond to external disruptions, most notably with the inclusion of historical characters that have disrupted the harmony of the community along with the religious symbols of the Catholic Church.

Of all influences on the cultural transformations of Bëtšknaté, the arrival of Spanish culture and Catholicism has been the most profound. As they came to the village, the conquistadors forced Kamëntšás to learn a new form of religious belief. Only if interpreted as a aesthetical dimension of life is the meaning of the dance now clear. Ugliness is exposed plain and simple along with the beautiful. Any interpretation that indicates that the dancing takes only one element is mistaken, as the aesthetic elements continue to be present and the philosophy of life remains alive. The aesthetic sensibility, which spurs the imagination of artists and musicians to create new artifacts for unification and forgiveness, cannot be taken away. Despite the fact that capitalist forms of exploitation have taken some of our arts, belts, and music to sell them in metropolitan cities, the aesthetic experience has not been taken away.

III. THE PHILOSOPHICAL SIGNIFICANCE OF KAMËNTŠÁ DANCING

My interpretation of Kamëntšás' dancing of forgiveness has been philosophically illuminated by the words of philosopher and poet Hartley Burr Alexander. In *The World's Rim*, Burr Alexander wrote that the Sun Dance of Native North Americans "is essentially an interpretation of life, of the meaning of nature for man, and of man's sense of his own human significance in the midst of nature—in short, of that which we call a philosophy of life."[20] I think Bëtšknaté is mainly a culturally aesthetic embodiment of the meaning of human existence.

Understood mainly as a celebration of recurring dichotomies of human existence, the Bëtšknaté allows us to appreciate our non-discursive ways of connecting with others and the rest of nature. At the beginning of *The Birth of Tragedy*, Friedrich Nietzsche indicated that a meaningful part of human life is lost when ceremonies and rituals are seen with the critical eye of reason, which sees in them nothing other than illusions or representations of festivities. The words of Nietzsche on the artistic Dionysian energies, impulses from nature that the Greeks actualized in their music and drama, fit quite well in the description of Bëtšknaté. "Under the charm of the Dionysian," writes Nietzsche, "not only is the union between man and man reaffirmed, but nature which has become alienated, hostile, or subjugated, celebrates once more her reconciliation with her lost son, man."[21] Later in his life, Ernst Cassirer also suggested that dancing is mimesis, which he qualified, saying that it is not a mere representation of the external world but also of the internal forces of the human being. He wrote: "Flute playing or dancing are, after all, nothing but imitations; for the flute player or the dancer represents by his rhythms men's characters as well as what they do and suffer."[22] Neither Nietzsche nor Cassirer, however, developed the notion of dancing as an enactment of collective aesthetic experiences. Against Cassirer, one can say that native dancing is more than a representation of subjective feelings. Philosophy of dancing might be a representation of dancing; yet, dancing itself is an enactment of the feelings and the emotions in a consummatory form, in the objective form of life as it comes. The ideas of John Dewey in *Art as Experience* allow us to see the fulfillment of the forces of nature through human creativity, despite that Dewey himself does not address native dancing as an example of aesthetic experiences but as the evolution of religious feelings.[23]

Dewey takes human experience to be the result of the interaction of an organism with its environment and art as the refined and intensified form of those experiences. From *Art as Experience*, one can see that Dewey's philosophy is an effort to trace a continuity between the basic elements of human experiences that come from the senses to the more refined, more symbolically charged kinds of experiences. Dewey's views are most useful to comprehend the philosophical significance of Bĕtsknaté in that they permit us to see the fulfillment of human experiences in aesthetics. Central to Dewey's philosophy is the idea of the mutual transformation of a living creature and its environment in the process of creating meaning. "The living creature," he says, "is exposed to dangers from its surroundings, and at every moment it must draw upon something in its surroundings to satisfy its needs. The career and destiny of a living being are bound up with its interchanges with its environment, not externally but in the most intimate way."[24] As a living culture, the Kamĕntsás have created aesthetic meaning from their own historical and cultural experiences, from interaction with other peoples.

On Dewey's view, the active capacity of an organism to modify its environment and the forces of the environment to modify its living organisms are the constituting elements of an experience. Like plants and animals, we have experiences; at once we transform the environment and are transformed by it. With the aid of our symbolic capacity to crystallize our experiences, we charge our doings and sufferings with meaning. We invest our energies intently, taking up that which affects us deeply. Art is the result of those intensified moments of our experience.

Properly understood, Bĕtsknaté condenses our native energies that emerged in the Sibundoy Valley. Insofar as our way of condensing our energies is through a dancing that symbolizes the underlying forces of our existence, we are affirming an aesthetic mode of existing that is not entirely discursive. In giving primacy to the feelings and emotions that evoke the side of humanity that refuses to be completely representational, the dancing gives a pause to the concern of the eternal modes of being to celebrate the modes of aesthetic existence, temporal, complex, challenging, and always recurring.

In addition to thinking of the mysteries of life, in the Kamĕntsá culture, we enact those forces of life through dancing, and we will continue to dance until we forget our place in the rest of the cosmos, until we forget that we have a special relation with *Tsbatsanamamá*. The dancing is the best aesthetic expression of our relationship with the cosmos, and our stopping is the sign of our alienation. Any attempt at understanding the meaning of Bëtšknaté in terms of the immediate perception of the beauty of clothes, of musical instruments, and of artifacts of peoples during the celebration is simplistic. The beauty lies elsewhere, in the capacity of the culture to celebrate the most fundamental concerns of its existence.

Nothing is more meaningful to the social life of a Kamëntšá or an Inga person than the participation in the dancing: only in the dancing are the vibrations of their hearts attuned spontaneously with the rest of the community and the rest of existence. Nothing touches more the emotional aspect of the Kamëntšá than the participation in a collective dancing that ritualizes the mixed feelings of alienation and self-reliance, of life-affirmation and death, of colonization and cultural survival. To use Dewey's language, Kamëntšá dancing is the intensified form of collective experience, the result of a prolonged and cumulative interaction with *Tsbatsanamamá*, Mother Earth.

IV. CONCLUSION

The celebration of Bëtšknaté is both a constituted and a constituting symbol of the Kamëntšá culture. It has a history that is condensed in different narratives and rituals, but its significance mainly lies in its constituting aspect, in that it provides aesthetic meaning. The ritual of forgiveness restores a unity of humans with the truly beautiful and with that which unifies us deeply, namely, with the act of recognition that we are members of the same family, all children of Mother Earth. Properly speaking, Bëtšknaté is a ritual of existence. It is the most beautiful experience a Kamëntšá or Inga person could have. It is, to paraphrase John Dewey's words in *Art as Experience*, the most refined and intensified form of collective experience of the natives of Sibundoy. It would be hard to find any other meaningful experience more collective and at the same time more personal to any Kamëntšá or Inga than this dance. It is personal in the sense that one's participation in the dancing comes from the need to reconnect with the rest of the families and to celebrate the cycles of life. As a native of Sibundoy, one cannot imagine oneself to be more beautifully prepared at any time other than in Bëtšknaté.

NOTES

1. Melvin Lee Bristol, "Sibundoy Ethnobotany" (PhD dissertation, Harvard University, 1965), 120.
2. "[La fiesta del perdón] marca el inicio del año indígena. Es el tiempo de preparar la tierra para el cultivo del maíz, pero también es el tiempo de reconciliación y del conjuro de las fuerzas colonialistas que llegaron con los españoles y se prolongaron con las misiones capuchinas." Omar Alberto Garzón Chivirrí, *Rezar, Cantar, Soplar: Etnografía de una Lengua Ritual* (Quito, Ecuador: Ediciones Ayba-Yala, 2004), 25.

3. Stanley Jeyaraja Tambiah, *Magic, Science, Religion, and the Scope of Rationality* (Cambridge: Cambridge University Press, 1990), 4.

4. In the introduction to *The Civilization of the South American Indians*, Krasten writes that his conclusions came from his stay among the Indians of the Argentine and Bolivian Gran Chaco in the years 1911 to 1913, and from a year residence among the savage or "half-civilized" tribes of eastern Ecuador in the years 1916 to 1919. Krasten's main purpose is to show that decorative purpose, "such as the painting of the face and the body, the cutting or shaving of the hair, the piercing of the lips and the ears for the insertion of the rings or other ornamental objects, the adorning and covering of the body with skins of animals, feathers of birds, or with necklaces, bracelets, and other ornaments, the wearing of masks, the mutilation of the body, as well as scarification and tattooing, that such and similar customs have not, in the first place, been practiced from decorative or aesthetic motives, but form part and parcel of the practical religion of the natives." Cfr. Rafael Krasten, *The Civilization of the South American Indians: With a Special Reference to Magic and Religion* (New York: Knopf, 1926), xiii.

5. In regard to Native North America, Thomas King and N. Scott Momaday have made explicit this double meaning of Land. Momaday wrote, "For obviously the Indian does use, and has always used, the land and the available resources in it. The point is that use does not indicate in any real way his idea of the land. Use is neither his word nor his idea. As an Indian I think, 'You say that I use the land, and I reply, yes, it is true; but it is not the first truth. The first truth is that I love the land; I see that it is beautiful; I delight in it; I am alive in it.'" Cfr. N. Scott Momaday, *The Man Made of Words* (New York: St Martin's Griffin, 1997), 40. Likewise, Thomas King wrote, "While the relationship that Native people have with the land certainly has a spiritual aspect to it, it is also a practical matter that balances with survival. It is an ethic that can be seen in the decisions and actions of a community and that is contained in the songs that Native people sing and the stories that they tell about the nature of the world and their place in it, about the webs and responsibilities that bind all things. Or, as the Mohawk writer Beth Brant put it, 'we do not worship nature. We are part of it.'" Cfr. Thomas King, *The Truth about Stories: A Native Narrative*, 1st ed. (Minneapolis: University of Minnesota Press, 2008), 113–14.

6. In 1965, Bristol noted that "the weaving of the colorful waist sashes worn by women is one of the more highly developed industries of the Sibundoy and is by far the highest form of artistic expression." Cfr. Bristol, "Sibundoy Ethnobotany," 31.

7. In addition to this conceptual distinction of land, family gardens, *jajañ*, in Kamëntšá language and *Chagra* in Inga, are taken as part of the family home.

8. McDowell observed that "Santiagueños living in Bogotá, Caracas, Panama City, or San José, Costa Rica, make every effort to return to the Sibundoy Valley for carnival season." John Holmes McDowell, *Sayings of the Ancestors: The Spiritual Life of the Sibundoy Indians* (Lexington: University Press of Kentucky, 1989), 10.

9. Bristol said that he finds it easy to converse over a bowl of chicha. "The natives were invariably friendly and often preferred to talk over a bowl of chicha." Cfr. Bristol, "Sibundoy Ethnobotany," vi. When I was a kid, to offer or to be offered chicha was a sign of hospitality. Except if one is sick, to refuse to drink chicha or to not offer it used to be a sign of disrespect.

10. McDowell, *Sayings*, 18–19.

11. Ibid.

12. Ibid.

13. Ibid.

14. Ibid.

15. Ibid., 62.

16. Justo Jacanamijoy España et al., *Camëntša Cabëngbe Ntšayanana* (Sibundoy: Uámana Soyënga Camëntšañe Uatsjéndayënga, 1994), 50.

17. I describe the meaning of winds in the next chapter, in discussion of the metaphysics of the rituals of healing.

18. As before indicated, the Ingas called the dancing "Atún Puncha," and their recorded memory also suggests cultural transformation over the years: (1) Cay carnavalta munanchi mi tucuycuna, tucuy pueblo. (2) Cay San andrés, Santiago, Sibundoy, Mucuga uray—chi amigocunas cayta munancuna mi cada huata. (3) Upiancuna mi bailajta. (4) Justiciapi cajpis, bailadero

mi cá banderahua. (5) Cunahora mana costumbre. (6) Yanga baillayla mi bailancuna—borrado "antigua costumbre"-ca. (7) Cayhóraca cucuruchu Parejo bailancuna yanga. (8) Ñujpatasina mana can chu. (9) Cunahora banderas chingarido mi cá. (10) Cucuruchu tia mí. [(1) We all wanted this festival—the whole town did. (2) San Andrés, Santiago, Sibundoy, down at Mocoa—all these friends wanted it, too, each year. (3) They drank and danced. (4) Even if they were office holders, they usually danced with the flag. (5) Now the custom is no more. (6) Now they just dance and have done away with the old custom. (7) Now the masked "devils" all dance. (8) It isn't like it used to be. (9) The flag is no more, too. (10) There are just the masked "devils."] Cfr. Stephen H. Levinsohn, *The Inga Language* (The Hague, Netherlands: Mouton & Co. B.V. Publishers, 1976), 111.

19. Part of our native prejudice against people of European descendent is that they do not really know how to dance. From this biased view, one tends to judge the beauty of European dances on the grounds of technically proficiency, as if they did not feel the dance but just followed dance steps mechanically.

20. Hartley Burr Alexander, *The World's Rim: Great Mysteries of the North American Indians* (Lincoln: University of Nebraska Press, 1953), 139.

21. Friedrich Nietzsche, *The Birth of Tragedy*, trans. Walter Kaufmann (New York: Vintage Books, 1967), 37.

22. Ernst Cassirer, *An Essay on Man* (New Haven, CT: Yale University Press, 1967), 138.

23. In *Art and Experience*, Dewey writes, "Dances and pantomime, the sources of the art of the theater, flourished as part of religious rites and celebrations." John Dewey, *Art as Experience* (New York: Penguin Group, 1934), 5.

24. Ibid., 12.

Chapter Three

Spirit in Kamëntšá Culture

The purpose of this chapter is to explain the symbolic framework that operates behind rituals of healing, with a particular emphasis on the yajé ritual as at present it is practiced in the lands of Sibundoy.[1] The main argument of the chapter is that the yajé ritual is both a constituted and constituting symbol of a culture that is based on a metaphysical worldview centered on wind ontology. In the Kamëntšá culture, winds take on a symbolic reality upon which rituals of purification and cleansing make sense. The rituals of cleansing and purification assume that there exists a symbolic construction of reality that affects the life of a Kamëntšá person. This symbolic construction of reality comes from the idea that winds are forces of nature that can affect the life of a person. This means that winds are not only physical but also metaphysical, in the sense that they carry negative and positive energies that affect the well-being of a person and the community. The negative and positive forces result from human interactions. The negative forces cause sickness, and the positive forces provide well-being. The origins of both positive and negative forces, according to the Kamëntšá culture, came from the forces of nature itself, but they become intensified with human action. Since those forces continue to be present, they cannot be ignored but rather must be faced with rituals. There are two main rituals.

The first is a ritual of cleansing; here, the patient does not have a personal encounter with the metaphysical reality but is only affected by it. The ritual of purification, on the other hand, comes when a person has an encounter with the metaphysical reality. The ritual of cleansing is to cure a person, to eliminate the negative forces of the person. The ritual of purification, on the other hand, is required when the person claims to have experienced a conscious encounter with powerful winds. The ritual of purification, therefore, requires the drinking of yajé, ayahuasca. It is here convenient to explain in detail the nature of these rituals.

I. NATIVE DOCTORS AND RITUALS OF HEALING: THE CONSTITUTED NATURE OF RITUALS

In the two cultures of the Sibundoy Valley, there are three types of doctors known as much for their moral character as for their efficacy in healing.[2] Equal in highest importance are the *tatšumbuás* and the *parteras*, both of whom are known for having received their healing gifts through some form of divine intervention more than through cultural training alone. Cultural training is necessary but insufficient to be a *tatšumbuá* or a *partera*. One can learn of some rituals of healing or diagnosis at home, but one cannot always have the power to heal. The community accepts as fact that some people have a gift, a power to heal.[3] The *tatšumbuás* specialize in healing ceremonies through yajé rituals. The *parteras* rule over the ritual of birth and the protection of women during pregnancy. While their knowledge of plants overlaps in some cases, *tatšumbuás* and the *parteras* each have some special capacities. Part of their reputation for wisdom consists in that they tacitly acknowledge their limitation and do not intervene in the rituals that others can enact better. *Tatšumbuás* disregard the presence of women menstruating in yajé ceremonies because during these times women are believed to have powers that deter any kind of wind, harmful or healing, making it difficult for a *tatšumbuá* to exercise the yajé healing ceremony.[4] In a similar manner, *parteras* repel the presence of people having taken yajé the day before a birth ceremony, as the newborn baby might receive harmful energies from the *tatšumbuás*' last patients or the woman giving birth might risk her life, suffering more than needed. As they both understand themselves to be on the same footing, and as both rituals consist ultimately of providing well-being for the community, *tatšumbuás* and *parteras* respect each other's rituals and do not interfere with one another.

Of secondary importance regarding healing practices are *Sobanderos, Sobanderas, Curanderos, and Curanderas*. These are people who provide first aid and specialize in treating spasms, minor frights, sprains, scrapes, and more "bodily" sicknesses. Their ability is believed to be the result of training and practice and less the result of divine inspiration, although in some cases they can also gain powers through divine intervention and become eventually *tatšumbuás* and *parteras*. Unlike *tatšumbuás* and *parteras*, these medical doctors of secondary importance can help patients affected by powerful winds, but when this is the case, their treatment is always palliative.

Among the Kamëntšá and Ingas, some people do have the powers not of healing but of causing harm. They are not considered medicine men and have no rank in the healing rituals. In Kamëntšá they are known as *yobang* and in Inga as *brujos*, or harmful people. The *yobang* are known for their mastery of harmful winds, which they learn through a slow cumulative process of resentfulness or envy. Because their power does not come as a gift to heal, the *yobang* are not as powerful as the *tatšumbuás*, and their tricks are easily challenged at home or with the drinking of yajé.

Of third importance concerning healing practices are all adult natives, especially mothers and fathers, although uncles and aunts without children are equally effective. Seijas refers to these types of healers as household curers; of them, she wrote, "The household curer operates within the context of the extended family; he treats cases of evil wind and non-mystical illnesses that are not regarded as serious. The therapeutic resources of household cures include curing performances as well as commonly known herbal remedies and patent drugs."[5] As a potential household curer, one learns from childhood of the effectiveness of specific plants and of the methods to detect whether a person is affected physically or metaphysically, even if one is not capable of healing patients completely. Usually, adults are prepared to distinguish whether a patient is physically or metaphysically sick. Except for nightmares, which are the surest signs of being the victim of metaphysical harming forces, adults' first approach to a patient is one of physical diagnosis. Common practices to detect if a patient suffers from physical diseases include talking with patients; asking about their dreams; seeing the patient's eyes; touching the forehead, the hands, and the stomach; and providing patients with an infusion of aromatic plants. Common ways to detect if a patient suffers from metaphysical disease include asking him or her about the last dream and eventually executing rituals of diagnosis. It is very difficult to detect whether a patient is physically or metaphysically sick if the patient is a child. In adults, it is relatively easy to diagnose and mitigate the pain.

The most apparent case of metaphysical sickness is a nightmare; in the absence of nightmares, there are two rituals of diagnosis. One of the most effective is rubbing oneself with pepper and throwing it into smoldering ashes. One can be sure to be affected metaphysically if the pepper cracks notoriously as soon as it is in contact with smoldering ashes. In Sibundoy, one learns early in one's childhood how to distinguish normal and abnormal cracking sounds of pepper in smoldering ashes.

Another ritual of diagnosis of metaphysical influences consists of spitting on a small cotton, wrapping it up, and throwing it on the floor. One can also be sure that one is metaphysically sick if the wrapped cotton becomes heavier than usual. Again, natives of Sibundoy can detect very quickly when a cotton wrap is more onerous than usual because of the sound it produces on contact with the floor. As before indicated, these rituals of diagnosis usually are performed when the patient does not indicate remembering his or her last dreams. While most trust in one of the rituals of diagnosis mentioned above, some people use both rituals to make sure that the patient is metaphysically affected. The "Vinỹ-wuasjanjaná," literally "whipped by the wind" but better translated as "the bad wind," is the most common manifestation of metaphysical disease, as it could act anytime with or without the about-to-be-victim's agency.

The basic ritual of treating metaphysical diseases at home takes two steps. First, one should burn aromatic plants and use their smoke to clean the sick person of bad winds; and second, one should call the person's name back, a calling that is a prayer to the winds and at the same time a ritual of restoration of the internal energies of a person. If the patient is metaphysically affected, this ritual of healing will relieve or at least produce a temporary relief for the patient. If the person relapses into the sickness, then the intervention of a *tatšumbuá* and the ritual of yajé is highly critical. Most native people interpret the ineffectiveness of this ritual of home healing as a sign that the patient suffers from a disease to be treated by a physician.[6]

Among the Kamĕntšás and the Ingas, dreams play a fundamental role in the life of an individual. Understood as signs connecting humans and their environment strongly, dreams function as warnings, subject to interpretations. Dreams orient the life of an individual and function differently depending on the context and the person who dreams. Some dreams foretell the fortune of a person disturbed or the tragedy of a family member. There is no direct cause-and-effect relationship between dreams and their content. At times, they function more as warnings.

Concerning sickness and healing, two types of dreams bear special significance. As it was mentioned in the chapter on storytelling, I indicated that dreams involving the chasing of bulls, cows, or horses or dreams of being visited by a nun or a priest are associated with bad winds. Ethnographic documentation suggests that this first type of dream took on a symbolic development with the arrival of the Spanish colonizers.[7] The second type of dream that warns a person of a metaphysical presence concerns the rising of rivers.[8] Documentation on rituals of healing and dream interpretation suggests that the spiritual forces of winds, either in their harming or healing manifestations, require some special rituals of healing.

II. SCHOLARLY DESCRIPTIONS OF YAJÉ

Scholars agree that yajé ceremonies emerged somewhere in the western Amazon, but they disagree on when and how they all started. Native voices naturally provide living testimonies of their knowledge and practices of their medicine, but these are generally taken as isolated personal testimonies that have no *objective* description with the *actual* history of the yajé ritual.[9] Jesuit priest José Chantre y Herrera is believed to be the first to have reported *evidence* of yajé ceremonies in the seventeenth century. While Chantre y Herrera reported yajé ceremonies more to warn the ecclesiastic authorities of the time of the practices of false religions than to describe their nature and significance, his report has served yajé scholars in disputing the history of yajé ceremonies. Eduardo Luna and Steven F. White, for example, criticize Chantre y Herrera for perpetuating the Eurocentric mentality that religious experiences that do not include the explicit recognition of the Catholic Church were the practices of "sorcerers" or "soothsayers."[10] Chantre y Herrera also contributed to seeing the yajé as a drug, insomuch as he labeled it an "infernal beverage"[11] used in ceremonies that invoke "the Demon." One can read Chantre y Herrera saying: "The science of divination consists simply in getting drunk, in having a face to speak lies shamefully, and in finding a way to decipher enigmas, all of which is not difficult to these barbarous and uncouth people."[12]

English botanist Richard Spruce is often cited as the second scholar to have reported on yajé ceremonies to the English world.[13] In the second half of the nineteenth century, Spruce traveled to different parts of the Amazon as an explorer and introduced an as-yet-unknown plant to the Western world. Spruce described the yajé as belonging to the family of *Malgiphiaceae* and to the genus of *Banisteria*. Surprised to have noticed the presence of an undescribed species at the time, Spruce took with him some living specimens in November 1853 and later classified it as *Banisteria caapi*, retaining the name partially given in Brazil and Venezuela. In his writings, he described the yajé plant as "woody twiner; stem thumb, swollen at joints. Leaves opposite, 6.4 x 3.3, oval acuminate, apiculato-acute, thinnish, smooth above, appresso-subpilose beneath."[14] In addition to *Caapi*, Spruce indicates that it had been named *Cadana* by the Tucano Indians on the Uaupés and *Aya-huasca*, meaning "dead man's vine," in Ecuador.

Spruce also reported that the lower part of the stem, smashed in a mortar with water and sometimes with a small portion of the other roots of the Caapi-pinima, is used to prepare the yajé beverage. "When sufficiently triturated," he says, "it is passed through a sieve, which separates the woody fibre, and to the residue enough water is added to render it drinkable. Thus prepared, its colour is brownish-green, and its taste bitter and disagreeable."[15] Spruce regrets he could not identify the "peculiar narcotic principle" that causes extraordinary effects. "Opium and hemp are its most obvious analogues," says Spruce, adding, "but Caapi would operate on the nervous system far more rapidly and violently than either."[16] In contact with other travelers of the time, Spruce also indicated that white men partaking of caapi reported to him to have similar experiences. Of those men, he wrote,

> They feel alternations of cold and heat, fear and boldness. The sight is disturbed, and visions pass rapidly before the eyes, wherein everything gorgeous

and magnificent they have heard or read of seems combined; and presently the scene changes to things uncouth and horrible. These are the general symptoms, and intelligent traders on the Upper Rio Negro, Uaupés, and Orinoco have all told me the same tale, merely with slight personal variations. A Brazilian friend said that when he once took a full dose of caapi he saw all the marvels he had read of in the Arabian Nights pass rapidly before his eyes as a panorama; but the final sensations and sights were horrible, as they always are.[17]

Spruce's travels and reports of these types of ceremonies have been confirmed by others who traveled to several parts of the Amazon and partook of a yajé ritual. Gerardo Reichel-Dolmatoff, considered the "father" of Colombian anthropology, has presented extensive ethnographic evidence of yajé ceremonies. Reichel-Dolmatoff wrote extensively on the Tukano people living in Vaupes in Colombia, with whom he shared a significant part of his life, trying to understand their worldview. Reichel-Dolmatoff wrote that in their original narrative of yajé, the Tukano people describe the yajé as a woman, as *gahpí mahsó*.[18] The story says that at the beginning of time, the Anaconda-Canoe was ascending the rivers to settle down humanity. At that time, the ancestors of all Tukano people were sitting inside of their first Maloca. The yajé woman showed up to the front of the Maloca and gave birth to her child, and then the story goes as follows:

> The woman walked toward the maloca where the men were sitting and entered through the door, with the child in her arms. When the men saw the woman with her child they became benumbed and bewildered. It was as if they were drowning as they watched the woman and her child.
>
> She walked to the center of the maloca and, standing there, she asked: "Who is the father of this child?"
>
> The men were sitting, and they felt nauseated and benumbed; they could not think anymore. The monkeys too, yes, the monkeys were sitting and were chewing herbs; they were bayapia leaves. The monkeys could not stand the sight either. They began to eat their tails. The tapirs, too, were eating their tails which, at that time, were quite long. The squirrels made a little noise—kiu-kiu-kiu—as it was chewing. . . .
>
> The yajé woman stood in the center of the maloca and asked: "Who is the father of this child?"
>
> There was a man sitting in a corner and saliva was dripping from his mouth. He rose, and seizing the child's right leg, he said: "I am his father!" "No!" said another man; "I am his father!" "No!" said the others; "We are the child's fathers!" And then all the men turned upon the child and tore it to pieces. They tore off the umbilical cord and the fingers, the arms, and the legs. They tore the child to bits. Each took a part, the part that corresponds to him, to his people. And ever since each group of men has had its own kind of Yajé.[19]

Unlike Spruce, Reichel-Dolmatoff offers a more meaningful narrative of a yajé ceremony in that the story emphasizes the unity and diversity of the yajé ceremony and its significance. The early medicine men, symbolized in the story as those who claimed parenthood of the child, might have had different experiences, but they all recognized that their wisdom comes ultimately from the same divine source, from a powerful infusing force that breaks down the fragmentary versions of the reality of the individuals and transforms them and makes them continuous.[20] While thinking stopped functioning before the divine woman, and humans and animals alike felt the overwhelming presence of the Divine, the ancestors interacted with the Divine and each claimed to have part of the Divine. No other explanation is more satisfactory when it comes to understanding the many communities that in different parts of the Amazon know of the use of yajé rituals.

At present, the diversification of yajé rituals beyond the Amazon region presents several challenges.[21] The once plant of the gods known only in the Amazon rainforest has now reached the streets of Colombia,[22] Buenos Aires, Paris, and the United States.[23] Europeans and Americans alike have also traveled to different regions of the Amazon to partake in the ritual, some later to become strong environmental, civic, and indigenous rights advocates, while others to become tragic symbols of negligence, taking the native medicine without the appropriate preparation.[24]

This challenging situation has called the attention of many scholars worldwide. Austrian medical ethnomusicologist Bernd Brabec de Mori, for example, has warned of the use of ayahuasca because of its doubtful historicity and because it is naïve to associate indigenous practices with paradisiacal solutions. De Mori criticizes the first report on ayahuasca by Chantre y Herrera, not on the grounds of Eurocentrism, but on the lack of evidence to affirm its history. Of Chantre y Herrera, De Mori says, "[Chantre y Herrera] describes a scene involving the ingestion of 'ayaguasca,' but he neither specifies year, place, or group of this observation, nor does he declare his source," and continues De Mori, "Note that Chantre y Herrera lived from 1738-1801. He never left Europe and his tome is compiled from secondary sources only."[25] Clearing the history of yajé, De Mori believes, would help yajé scholars take a more critical stance on whether they are treating a recent phenomenon that might demand a more careful investigation or whether they are addressing an ancient religious practice. Before an international conference on the globalization of ayahuasca at the Center for the Psychosocial Medicine of Heidelberg University in 2008, De Mori disputed the claim that ayahuasca had emerged in the Peruvian Amazon and that it had been used before the arrival of the Spanish conquest. In his published speech, De Mori claims he does not dispute the qualities of ayahuasca use or its meaning to indigenous people, but he insists that we should be aware of the possibility that ayahuasca usage might become a *drug* problem in the global context. As he wrote it, De Mori wanted at once to challenge the idea that old does not mean valuable and new does not mean bad when it comes to evaluating indigenous practices. He also wanted to make scholars aware of the fact that ayahuasca does not heal everything.[26]

In challenging the lack of evidence of the millennial use of ayahuasca, De Mori wanted anthropologists and ethnohistorians to think more carefully about the nature of their investigations. He wanted them to know whether they are investigating "a hallucinogenic drug that was spread relatively recently through Catholic missions and by rainforest mestizos," or whether they are researching a "traditional remedy that has been used by forest Indians for at least five thousand years." "The crucial point," says De Mori, "is not what anthropologists and ethnohistorians think about the issue, but rather the opinion held by the public, the drug and biopiracy policy, and in the end, even by some research founders."[27] In other words, De Mori believes that knowing the history of ayahuasca usage will offer insights about public policies regarding the internationalization of ayahuasca and the extent to which it would affect our ideas about drugs. He also intentionally skipped indigenous accounts of the history of yajé ceremonies because he believes that indigenous peoples using ayahuasca assert their knowledge of the plant to make political and historical arguments. He says, "Indigenous protagonists often use references to pre-Columbian roots as a (well-working) strategy to obtain a stronger position in the globalizing world."[28] It should be here noted that De Mori's conclusions are based on his fieldwork in Peruvian lowlands, with a special interest in ethnomusicology in the Ucayali Valley, in which, according to De Mori, "the use of ayahuasca is probably less than 300 years old."[29]

The scholarship on the spiritual life of the Sibundoy Valley concerning yajé rituals is mostly descriptive. The yajé ritual has been studied more out of curiosity for the chemistry of the plant and less for an investigation on the meaning and value that it creates. Meaning and value creation has been studied in terms of narratives, not in terms of rituals of healing. The first scholarly account of rituals of healing comes from the work of Melvin Lee Bristol.

Bristol was a student of Richard Evans Schultes, who had changed the conversation on the investigation of narcotic plants. As an experimentalist and traveler, Schultes had visited the Sibundoy Valley and found a species of *Dantura* that was used in rituals of healing. As a graduate student at Harvard University, Bristol became interested in knowing the nature and story behind the *Dantura*, a hallucinatory plant that, according to Schultes and later confirmed by Bristol, has developed interesting mutations in the Sibundoy Valley. Investigating this plant, Bristol became more and more interested in the accounts that the natives of Sibundoy would make of some of the plants. While he had visited the Sibundoy Valley in 1960, in 1963 he decided to stay in Sibundoy for two years with his wife and daughter, carrying out his doctoral dissertation on the plants of Sibundoy and their special significance for the people. "Sibundoy Ethnobotany," Bristol's dissertation, offers a detailed description of the plants and their use among the natives of the Sibundoy Valley. Classifying them according to their use, the explanation of rituals based on medicinal plants that he offers is very limited. He comments that "the presence of aroma in a plant implies medicinal value" and "all known medicinal plants are thought to be aromatic and any other plants found to have an aroma are supposed to have medicinal value even if no one has yet discovered their correct therapeutic application."[30] But he does not offer a detailed explanation of the meaning of the rituals of healing with plants. Nor is he interested in describing the symbolism of winds common in yajé rituals of healing or purification. His interests are more in the plants themselves and less in the relation between plants and humans. While he dedicates some pages to describing the ritual use of the yajé plant in Sibundoy, his descriptions are more of an outside observer than of an inside drinker, so to speak. He wrote that he did not experience himself the transformative, religious effects of the plant. He said that his experience remained on the physical level.[31]

The second approach to yajé as practiced in the lands of Sibundoy comes from another scholar, Haydée Seijas. Following the works of Bronislaw Malinowski, Seijas offers a more robust interpretation of the rituals of healing and rituals of purification of the Sibundoy Valley. Her dissertation, titled "The Medical System of the Sibundoy Indians of Colombia," accounts for two kinds of diseases: mystical and physical. She refers to the mystical as "unusual in some way," as opposed to the clear source of physically caused diseases. While the purpose of her dissertation is to account for the "non-mystical types of diseases," she also writes extensively on how winds play an important role. Because of her commitment to explaining naturally caused diseases, Seijas interprets "evil winds" as an example of *susto*, or fright,[32] emphasizing thereby the natural cause of a disease. Her approach to the Sibundoy medical system comes as a reaction to the anthropological literature of the time when she was writing. As she wrote in 1969, "While anthropological literature abounds in accounts of beliefs in the mystical causation of illness and concomitant practices, little or no attention has been devoted to beliefs in 'natural' or non-mystical causes of disease."

Like Bristol's account, Seijas's remains on the level of description; it is not an account of meaning. The most obvious example to illustrate that she does not want to be involved in the discussion on the meaning of the rituals that she describes is that she does not delve into the meaning of the ritual of purification nor into the nature of the medicine man administering yajé. She does not provide any account of the belief that one cannot be a medicine man if one does not receive in one or another form a gift from the divine. "Among the Sibundoy there is no special call; no physical or psychological characteristic signals or compels a person to become a medicine man," writes Seijas. And she continues,

> Although it is generally stated that with the appropriate training anyone may become a medicine man, there is a tendency for sons of medicine men to adopt their fathers' specialty. It is also said that the trade can be learned from local medicine men, and no doubt the sons of medicine men who choose to become specialists learn a great deal from their fathers. However, in order to be fully recognized as such, a medicine man must get his training from specialists of lowland groups, such as the Tukanoan, Koreguaje, Makaguaje and Siona, or the Quechua speaking groups of the Caquetá and the Putumayo river basins. . . . Formal training in the lowlands is started at about sixteen or seventeen years of age. The length of the training varies, but it usually takes more than one year of continuous residence with the teacher, and some say that up to six years of training are necessary.[33]

Such a description disregards the spiritually transforming capacity of the medicine man. Several accounts of personal engagement with the spirit of the yajé cannot be limited to an explanation of cultural training. Central to someone being a *tatšumbuá* (medicine man) is that the powers to heal others come from a gift from the divine and are not solely based on cultural training. To be sure, cultural practice is necessary but insufficient to become a *tatšumbuá*.

As I indicated in chapter 2 of this work, after staying more than two years with the Inga people of San Andrés and Santiago, McDowell offered an interpretation of the spiritual life of the Sibundoy Valley based on dream interpretation of the locals. McDowell starts his book, *Sayings of the Ancestors: The Spiritual Life of the Sibundoy Indians*, with the promising thesis that dream interpretation in the Sibundoy Valley does not indicate superstition but rather suggests the presence of a folk religion having an internal logic.[34] Both from conversation with his native informants and from careful observation, McDowell indicates that the sayings of the ancestors are the result of indigenous interpretations of the presence of spiritual energies in dreams and wakeful states. As I also indicated in previous chapters, McDowell's theoretical framework does not explain the rituals of healing and diagnosis, nor does he explain the ontology of the winds that underlie all the rituals of metaphysical healing. His interpretation is limited to the narrative structures of the locals.

What all this scholarship indicates is that the ritual of yajé is neither unique nor specific to the Sibundoy Valley. All scholars agree that the yajé emerged in the Amazon. Despite its origins, the yajé rituals in Sibundoy have become a fundamental part of the culture, one that provides spiritual meaning and speaks of the human need to create a metaphysical or spiritual sense of life. The experience of the holy might be different in different cultures, but the cultural embodiment in Sibundoy in terms of rituals of healing and purification through yajé means that the symbolic quest for meaning takes a spiritual, more personalized dimension of life. Of these kinds of experiences, I now turn my attention.

III. YAJÉ CEREMONIES IN SIBUNDOY: THE CONSTITUTING ASPECTS OF YAJÉ

In addition to my first encounter with yajé to which I referred in the preface to this work, an experience that pushed me to think about existence and meaning and eventually led me to the sinuous fields of philosophy, I participated in other yajé rituals, not all pleasant but all of them significant. Here I want to limit myself to describing some of the most significant ones.

My first story is of the time when I was a young adult and had just started college. During vacation time, my sister and I used to visit my grandfather because he was funny and inspirational at once. I have no memory of him teaching us what he knew. In fact, he used to be evasive when asked about his healing powers or his past experiences. Smiling, he would say, "I do not remember anything of my past because I was born not long ago, and I came into the world as an adult, as you see me today." When pressed to answer in a more serious way, he only referred to it as a gift from God. My sister, more curious than I, once asked him to tell us more about his medicinal powers, and he agreed to tell us what he remembered. "When I was about fourteen, I participated in a yajé ritual, for the first time," he started, once he realized that he could not avoid the curiosity of my older sister. And then he continued,

> Very often I used to help my father carrying out beans, taro, maize, or fruits from our *jajañ* [native garden] to trade with the people of *Šhatjoy* [the lowlands of Putumayo, i.e., Mocoa]. It used to be a trip of twelve hours' walking. Among my father's traders was an old wise-looking man who once invited us to join a yajé ritual with a group of people. Two or three of the man wearing special clothes remained close to a small table where one could see different dry leaves. The rest were sitting rather quietly. As they saw us, they spoke in their own language, and then they invited us to sit, talking to my father in Kamsá and Inga. I remember that I was given a small drink, like a *cuaštem* [a very small cup used to share drinks], and the next memory is of my father waking me up to eat something and asking me to prepare for our way back to Sibundoy.
>
> On our way back to Sibundoy, my father told me not to speak of this ritual with my relatives. I continued to live like all people; I kept working with my father, got married when I was in my twenties, and had to work hard because my father sold the land he had to the whites and left us without land heritage. Because of my work and because I knew the road to *Šhatjoy*, I traveled several times to trade the products of my *jajañ* or to legalize the land that I bought. In

one of these trips for trading, I had a very intimate experience that remained dear to me. The oldest of my sons, your father, could not join me because he was sick, I believe.

Because I had an agreement with *Shatjoyëng* [the people of Mocoa] to bring them my products, I once departed from Sibundoy early in the morning. I might've walked about six hours or so when it started to rain. Gradually it became a storm, with powerful winds, thunder, and lightning turning the sky gray and the mountains dark. I had to stop walking, get myself out of the road, and seek refuge under a rock. I patiently waited, but it continued to get darker and darker, and the raining caused several small creeks by my side. I was trying to see if there could be a safer place when I saw a small lightning rock [*binÿetšá*] in one of the small rivers, just a few steps from where I was. I saw it for a little while. It looked beautiful, shining in the middle of the frightening night and slowly being clothed by water. As it was the only shining element in the dark mountain, I moved quickly to take it, and when I made it, it slowly stopped raining.

When I met my *Shatjoyëng* friends, without me telling what had happened on the road, they invited me to another yajé ceremony. When I had another drink of yajé, I remained partially conscious, in a state where I was not quite sure if the people who I saw praying and singing in colorful clothes were my friends or if they were others who came in just for the night. It is even more difficult to say what precisely happened because I could not remember everything. I do remember that the day after this incident my friends advised me to keep the crystal quartz as much protected as I could because it was a gift from God so that I can use it for healing.[35]

At once afraid and encouraged about what happened, I returned to Sibundoy, but nothing changed in my life. I continued to work for my family on the farm, and very often I had to pawn part of my lands to have loans from the small bank that came into Sibundoy in order to have enough land for all my children. My visits to *Shatjoy* continued twice a year. I started to realize that I must use the medicine powers when you and other of my grandchildren started to get sick unexpectedly.

My knowledge of plants came from the interaction with *Shatjoyëng* and from my rituals wherein I had the opportunity to see what plants I should and should not use. Sometimes I had been asked about how to become a medical man, and my answer has always been the same. As I did not choose to train myself to be a medical doctor, but what I know came to me in the form of revelation, I always invoke God for his guidance, inspiration, and protection.

When I do not see that I can heal them, I let people know that they should look for another person or the white doctors. What I do know is that some plants have the power to heal and they are very effective if you know how to use them. Unfortunately, in part because of our ignorance of plants and in part because we use our lands more and more for becoming rich, we tend to forget.[36]

As the story reveals, for my grandfather it was clear that the knowledge of plants came from cultural interaction whereas the power of healing came as a gift. As he was a Catholic, in his rituals he prayed in Kamëntšá, Inga, and

Spanish. He was careful to emphasize that he had been blessed with power because of his dedication to work and to helping others. The story indicates that for my grandfather the yajé ceremony had a special religious significance. My grandfather did not want to share his story, in part because he knew that its importance might not be understood. He also was reluctant to tell the story because he was aware that the content of his story was not any different from stories that other people create in order to claim falsely to have healing powers. When asked about the difference between "real" and "false" doctors, my grandfather used to say that a person is known through her actions. A real doctor knows not only how to heal but also does not use the medicine to cause damage to others. To his understanding, if one claims to be divinely inspired, one cannot cause harm to others. As inspirational as this story was to me at the time, I did not understand its significance fully until later in my life when I partook in another yajé ritual with another medicine man, almost three years after the death of my grandfather. When he was alive, my grandfather allowed me to participate in many rituals. I slowly learned to appreciate more fully the power of transformation through yajé rituals. In my learning process, however, I harbored doubts about the powers of the yajé.

My second story dates to the time when I was a junior in college and became a skeptic of the powers of yajé. If yajé had such powers to heal and bring about well-being to the community, how, I used to ask myself, could I reconcile the idea that there is a spiritual power in the yajé when its beneficial effects do not yield any benefits to the community at large? Not only had I witnessed the rise of young native suicides but also the high rates of alcoholism in youth. I started to see that my generation carried a yoke of poverty that led some of my friends to suicide, desolation, and alcohol addiction. Because I already had gone through similar forms of thinking, I used to wonder why our medical doctors, powerful as they claimed to be, did not help to prevent us from experiencing or thinking about those tragic consequences. Why had the medicine men, I wondered, become powerless in the face of constant land exploitation? How, I used to ask myself during nights of insomnia, could someone reach higher powers to heal and improve the lives of others without at the same time being able to improve his own economic circumstances? Overwhelmed with those questions, I used to wander and read more about other experiences of yajé rituals, though in general I disliked most of the reports of anthropologists who described their experiences because they portrayed an image of natives living in unrealistic paradisiacal environments, caring after each other with almost sublime innocence. I even doubted whether they really traveled and lived or just fantasized about the image of the native as the noble savage that Rousseau had inspired.

While I did not confess my skepticism openly to anyone, my readings led me to conversations and interactions with people from other areas of study. I met someone who had just finished his bachelor's in clinical psychology and had been borrowing almost the same books that I had been checking out. We met in a university library in Manizales and talked more in detail about our mutual concerns after a coffee. Having indicated that he also had been puzzled by different reports he had heard, he told me he would like to visit my grandfather, if possible. I took him to my village one day, and after a brief introduction to my grandfather, we entered my grandfather's room where he healed and practiced his rituals.

My grandfather told us that he could only help us with a ritual of cleaning but not with a ritual of purification because he did not have the adequate medicine. The difference between these two rituals is that in the former the patient does not embark on a metaphysical trip, while in the latter careful preparation and disposition to journey with the mind is necessary. Disappointed that my grandfather did not have his medicine and moved by my skepticism, I made a terrible mistake.

After my grandfather performed the ritual of cleaning and told my friend he needed to reexamine his life because his energies remained in disarray, he went to the kitchen to bring us some food. I used this opportunity to ask my friend how he felt, and he said that there was something in my grandfather that made him wise, in part because he had told a truth that my friend knew but had refused to admit to himself. My friend also commented on his disappointment to know that my grandfather did not have the other medicine for which we were looking. As I noticed that my grandfather was still in his kitchen, I took the bottle of the medicine that he had just used to clean my friend, and I drank it, just to know how one could feel the other effects of yajé. I wanted to know whether yajé could destroy my will not to embark on a journey and whether it really had the power that I had been told it had. I wanted to prove to myself that if I remained in control of myself, I would not be taken anywhere in my mind. I thought that I could challenge the extent to which yajé depended ultimately on mere psychological disposition, which one could decide not to have. I also convinced my friend that he should drink a bit, less than what I drank. When my grandfather came back to the ritual room, he conversed with us and asked my friend more of his travels.

After making our excuses, we exchanged good-byes with my grandfather, and he invited us to come back at another time. On our way home, my friend told me that he felt the power of my grandfather when he looked at him in the eyes and that what he said during his cleaning ritual was true. My friend left Sibundoy the same day, and I remained in my hometown until the next day, waiting to travel with my older sister. Never would I forget my experience of the next day.

Everything was normal for the first two hours of traveling from Sibundoy to Manizales. After about two hours, I felt dizzy and tried to sleep, hoping to restrain myself from puking. The sneaky roads, climbing up the Andean mountains, did not help. Each time the bus would turn to ascend a bit, I felt a contortion in my stomach. As we were traveling at night, my sister gave me water and some pills to help me out. But it was in vain. I was fully conscious of my stupidity and had no other option other than to pray without saying what happened to anyone else.

I vomited for about nine hours in a trip of fourteen hours, my sister in vain trying to help me. Some of my friends who traveled with us initially made fun of me, suggesting that this happens to the native that goes to the city and forgets to drink *chicha*. But later almost everyone was worried about my condition. My grandfather probably knew about my condition, but there was nothing much he could do either. At dawn the next morning I slowly recovered myself. In the minds of a non-native, this episode could be reinterpreted as a mere biological condition. True to my experience is that this was the result of a necessary punishment of yajé itself.

My third story refers a meaningful and transformative moment in my life. After my grandfather died, I almost did not want to drink yajé anymore. After I was about to complete my master's thesis, in December 2012, I went with my sister to visit an old medicine man of the neighboring Inga people. I remembered this to be my best experience, one in which I felt the presence of my grandfather, and I here proceed to provide more details of a yajé ceremony.

Like the ceremony with my grandfather, this time the Inga medicine man started about 9 p.m. I had prepared myself as my grandfather used to suggest to me. The yajé drinking ritual requires the careful daylight preparation of the mind and body of the drinker with the purpose of creating the conditions for tuning the drinker's finite nature with the unconditioned nature, with that which manifests itself once a sacred dose of yajé is taken. At night, after the due daytime preparation, the drinker partakes in one cleaning ritual before the yajé ritual. The person to be drinking should try to remain in silence, in a meditative mood, not thinking about daily-life occupations, but being sensitive to higher levels of reality, trying to understand life's purposes and necessities.

Walking in a state of wonder at the beauty of silence in the *jajañ* (native garden) is perhaps the best way of preparing oneself for the yajé ritual of purification. This meditative practice, not highly cultivated in societies driven primarily by the force of industry and money-making, requires temporary detachment from responsibilities. It is a formal process of undoing habituation to find a balance between one's energies and those of the universe. A well-cultivated *jajañ* condenses cosmic energies, its plants constantly exuding refined good winds. Walking in the *jajañ* is an activity of pausing our daily-life activities to enter into a realm of possibilities, like Husserl recommended the Europeans should do when they seemed to have forgotten to live humanly. Through their own experiences, the medicine men have experienced the enslaving sense of attachment that humans endure in the process of habituation to their own finite nature, which often leads them to disavow the reality of the infinitely greater nature.[37] This process of habituation to the finite nature makes the human mind feel at home in the most concrete and the most finite of the ways of being, leading us to busy ourselves in the understanding of fragmented realities, neglecting their transiency when compared with spiritual existences. A close preparation for the yajé ritual of purification, my grandfather used to tell me, makes us aware that the finite could not exist without the infinite, that everything is interrelated to form clusters, spirals of energy, like those one sees in the journey to the spiritual realm. I had gone thus prepared for the ceremony with the Inga medicine man.

That night the Inga medicine man followed the same steps that my grandfather used to do. In the ritual room, he had a candle and all the sacred instruments used for the ritual of cleaning and for the ritual of purification.[38] The ritual of cleaning is a preparation for entering the spiritual realm clean. It consists of cleaning the body and the mind for a trip to the spiritual world, to the world in which one can feel the reality of winds. Invoking the powers of the wind with the sacred broom[39] and praying to God and the ancestors, my medicine man started with the ritual of purification, asking me to repeat my name as he prayed to the winds, to the ancestors, and to God, conjuring thereby my drink. Once my drink was conjured, he gave me the drink and told me not to drink it yet. I took the small bowl, silently made my intentions and purposes clear, blew slowly three times over the yajé drink, and then I returned it to him for the second conjuration. Taking the sacred broom and sweeping the bad winds off my body, he again called to the spirit of the yajé to come back, singing, first slowly and then more intensely. After this, he placed the drink on a small table and covered it up, and as if the situation were not sacred, he changed the conversation to trivial matters. I suddenly felt that I was talking to an American acquaintance whom I met in an elevator, for we talked about the weather and how everything looked interesting. When I became more engaged in the conversation, the medicine man, changing again the conversation, asked me if I was ready. With a strong sense of reverence for the yajé this time, I said yes, and I drink the small portion of yajé.

About twenty minutes after I drank yajé, the sounds of the night that had once seemed like any other to me became as recognizable as the voices of old friends. Suddenly, I was hearing the sternal melody that my grandfather used to make in his rituals. It became a peaceful music, a suggestive invitation to walk away from the shades of fear. Never had I experienced the flux of discrete events passing by my mind. They are always entangled with my present, unpredictable as my response to the utterly unexpected. At times I felt overpowered by entwined memories, their meanings as elusive as my childhood experiences of estrangement, which I sometimes used to have when a relaxing night stroll in my mother's *jajañ* would turn into a hard effort to free myself from thickets of entangled lianas. Sometimes I felt that the lianas' strong and thorny threads gradually tightened me to big trees, making useless any of my movements until a gentle wind in the silence of the night would caress the leaves and tendrils of those big trees, its soothing force untangling the lianas, leaving me free to walk back home. Never have I tried to exhaust the utter meaning of those experiences, as enough satisfaction I have found in considering them my personal, symbolic attachments to Mother Earth. Then I could only see shadows, the outline of objects that I could not fully determine. The music of my grandfather was gradually dissolving the shadows, turning them into present objects with coherent unity, as events, their vivacity reversing my sense of the real and the imaginary, making me feel that I had an attachment to some deeper forces of which I was previously unaware.

Now that I return from my experiences of yajé ceremonies and I put those memories down, my mind takes me back to that night, to the vivid imagery of my closed eyes seeing colorful spiral patterns of clouds moving in the sky, turning gently into big and small rainbows. These big rainbows, in turn, brought about imageries of myself walking through muddy roads. Then they led me to a peaceful path, enclosed by big, colorful trees, their constant movement transforming them into grotesque spirals of clouds, much like those one could see before tornados. This imagery was so disturbing that I could not avoid a bothering sensation arising from my stomach to my mouth, forcing me to recall the most painful of my vomiting experiences. And then I would remember the small rainbows that would graciously move, their bright colors gradually fading, slowly merging into the darker colors to form then the heart and the veins of the leaves of green trees. The trees, maintaining the flux of energy, would widen themselves, creating roads, inviting me to listen to the dim sounds of hummingbirds.

It was probably about three in the morning when I felt that I needed to sleep because it was getting cold. My sister who had been watching me had been concerned about my condition. Asked how I felt, I told her that despite how miserable I might have looked that night, I had a truly beautiful experience and that I only needed some time to sleep.

The next day I felt like I had been born again. I have heard experiences like the one here described. True to my life is that the writing of my own experiences made me aware that I had indeed participated in the symbolic representation of a native conception of the universe, which I now proceed to explicate.

IV. WIND SYMBOLISM AND METAPHYSICS OF HUMAN EXISTENCE

As I explained it in chapter 2, the natives of Sibundoy think of their natural environment, of the plants, animals, and all existing things, as a large home, like a small cosmos. The Sibundoy Valley is charged with symbols of life and death, with encouraging and disturbing memories, with signs of hope and tragedy. Winds are conceived as the unifying, the grounding forces of physical and symbolic manifestations of all existence. In addition to their material manifestations in the form of gusts, the Sibundoy winds have a symbolic dimension, a way of being that is not necessarily positive or naturally good. As symbolic forces, they transcend their own materiality and become harmful or healing, affecting the life of natives of Sibundoy. Native doctors look for material manifestations of spiritual forces, however elusive they might be. A fright, a sudden electric pulse of part of the body, or a sudden feeling of a gust in one's walking are the most common material manifestations of harmful winds, each requiring the intervention of native doctors in the calling after positive energies.

My main thesis in this section is that dream interpretation, rituals of healing, and especially yajé ceremonies as they are practiced in Sibundoy cannot be comprehended without an ontology of the winds. The ontology of the winds is my characterization of the framework that works behind the rituals of healing and which I have constructed on a careful reflection on the cultural experience of my people. Every native in Sibundoy feels the presence of certain types of winds and understands them as primary manifestations of something beyond the mere physical gust. Kaměntšás and the Ingas share the view that winds unify the physical and the spiritual domains of the world. Although physical gusts, they belong to a domain different from the physical; they belong to a spiritual domain, a domain of cultural memory and imagination that has some independence of the existence of individuals but that yet interacts constantly with the life of the community. This spiritual domain harbors the cumulative experiences of the ancestors, their doings, their sufferings, and their hopes. Actions, places, or names of ancestors that have benefited or caused harm to the community transcend the specific individual who caused them and become energies. The actions of current individuals who help others, especially those of men and women who have powers of healing, become crystalized as healing energies for new generations.

Negative energies are crystallizations of the harming actions of ancestors, of present generations, and of past and present experiences of sufferings. They too may be called upon, but to cause harm. The invoking of actions, places, or names of ancestors who have caused harm to the community activates the forces of pain in victims of the present. Freely moving through rivers, forests, stones, and mountains, winds can absorb the negative feelings of people and can turn into bad winds. The clearest example often commented among Kamëntšás is the case of a person who harbors envy or thinks badly of another person. If the envious person dedicates a lot of time to thinking badly of another person, the air that comes while so thinking becomes bad wind. If this wind is strong enough or the victim does not take precautions, it can cause severe physical damage in the person. Other types of bad winds emerge from places where people died and were not buried appropriately or where their families did not pay due respect. As these are historical, they form more powerful winds that require the intervention of native doctors to heal.[40]

This allure to the winds has led Kamëntšás and Ingas alike to understand themselves as tied intrinsically to their place of origin. Winds, called *Vinÿë* in Kamëntšá and *huayra* in Inga, are the physical manifestations of the native soul of the Sibundoy Valley, as Kamëntšá poet Hugo Jamioy wrote in 2010, "Quem uábeman endmën binÿbe oyebuambnayán"[41] ("Our poetic voices are the voices of the wind"). When a wind causes spiritual harm to a person, it has become a *Vinyiaj* (in Kamëntšá) or *huayra sacha* (in Inga), a sickly wind. We say in Kamëntšá that a person is *Vinÿe Wansjanjaná* if the person is whipped by a bad wind. If a person knows the prayers and the ritual to heal a person sick of bad winds, it is not necessary to go to a native doctor, except if the person relapses. Otherwise, a native doctor is the best option. If not taken care of properly, the *Vinÿe Wansjanjaná* (the person sick because of a bad wind) might be severely affected and eventually could die. It is easy to know if a person is *Vinÿe Wansjanjaná* because bad winds produce nightmares, unexpected electric pulses on the body of the affected, or sudden sickness. It is easier to heal when the manifestation is immediate. When the winds go deep enough into the spiritual life of a person, it is more difficult, for in that case the bad winds produce nightmares.

The ontology of the winds then explicates how harmful and beneficial energies affect the well-being of individuals and of the community at large. This ontology is assumed in the rituals of healing, and it clearly is experienced in the yajé ritual of purification. Yet, and more importantly, the ontology of winds accounts for that intimate relation that humans develop with their environment. One might object that the most intimate relation of the natives of Sibundoy rests on symbolic meaning that the land represents. Thus, one might bring into the conversation the idea that the land is at once a place to use, *fšants* in Kamëntšá, and the mother of all existing things in Sibundoy, the *Tsbatsanamamá* (Mother Earth). And one might suggest that the most fundamental kind of relation is not based on winds but on the land. If such might be an objection to my articulation here, I would respond in two ways: first, while the symbolic conception of land (*Tsbatsanamamá*) accounts for a meaningful relation that the native cultures establish with the origin of all existing things, this symbolic relation is not charged with the meaning of mental and physical health that the ontology of winds explains. As I explained in chapter 2, the symbolic relation that comes from *Tsbatsanamamá* and the native culture speaks of aesthetic fulfillment with respect to harmony and natural beauty of the space and the people. Winds account for the relation of the native and his or her experiences of health and holiness. Second, even if one wants to take the symbolic meaning of land to be more fundamental to the cultural experience, I think one cannot make sense of the experience of health and holiness merely from the symbolic representation of land. One needs, at least in principle, an explicative framework to make sense of the symbolic meaning of the winds.

It might further be objected that ultimately one can reduce the spiritual dimension, which includes health and the holy, into the aesthetic dimension, on the grounds that the annual dancing also speaks of the intimate relation of the humans with their natural surroundings. I think such an objection does not do justice to the personal relationship that one achieves with the holy through yajé rituals. Bĕtšknaté accounts for the relation between humans and Nature (*Tsbatsanamamá*) in a collective form. Yajé rituals account for the relation between humans and winds in a more personal form.

The binding connection between the spiritual and the physical realm through winds suggests that when a native person becomes forgetful of her roots, of the memories of ancestors, and of the possibilities of actualizing further symbolic representations of life, that person suffers alienation. Sibundoy rituals of healing do not make sense in other places because they are rooted to the specific place. They are meaningful in the place of origin and for the people who came to the place to share parts of their lives. Kamĕntšás and Ingas are aware that in other places, other people root their core beliefs in different symbolic representations. In Sibundoy, we have centered our systems of beliefs in winds.

V. CONCLUSION

In this chapter, I provided a brief description of the rituals of healing and the ritual of purification through yajé. I argued that the yajé ritual is both a constituted and a constituting symbol of the Kamĕntšá culture; I showed that it is constituted in the sense that it works as a ritual requiring preparation, guidance, and disposition. One of my stories suggested that drinking yajé without preparation or without the guidance of a medicine man is not only naïve, but it could also be dangerous. Its effectiveness is contingent upon the cultural context and works within the framework of the special relation that native cultures have developed historically with their natural environment. I also suggested that the yajé ritual functions as a constituting symbol in that it provides spiritual fulfillment and is transformative.

I also explained that the yajé ritual of purification and other rituals of healing presuppose a conception of the world, a world that has positive and negative energies. While at present there are no stories of the personifications of winds, it seems clear that the rituals presuppose a spiritual world that houses positive and negative winds and that interacts with humans. They do not become negative or positive only in relation with a community of the present. As I demonstrated, negative energies also come from the community of the past, and the actions of the present might become positive or negative. Evidence of humans having negative winds is the fragility and propensity to forget the purpose and meaning of living as humans and in harmony. Evidence of positive energies lies in the human capacity to heal, recover, and forgive.

The ontology of winds not only explicates the rituals of healing and purification but also accounts for a more symbolic, spiritual element in the human mind. The rituals of healing that all adults learn suggest that the capacity and disposition to seek a meaningful life is present in each human being. But they also account for the human capacity to destroy, to cause harm to the present and to the future. Over generations, the natives of Sibundoy have considered some plants to have magic powers, not so much because of their mysterious way of behaving in different persons, but because they have powers that reorient the life of an individual and provide to him or her a variety of options that he or she has not seen before. The yajé plant is magical not because it creates alternative realities, but because it has the power to actualize the possibilities of human existence that cannot be otherwise seen. Some may need the ritual once in their lives; others might not need it. But so long as the quest for meaning is a human need that cannot be avoided and if one is born in a land charged with symbolic meaning, one cannot avoid participating in the yajé ritual, in the same way one learns of the beginnings of the culture through storytelling, and in the same way one learns of the value of beauty in the dancing. People of other latitudes might find it meaningful to orient themselves through readings, writings, and material commodities. Kaméntšás have learned to create and understand the meaning of human life and existence at large through oral tradition, dancing, and rituals.

One might ask finally why it is worth accounting for a native conception of the world. What if this is all superstition, one might wonder; anthropologist Wade Davis has an insightful answer. He writes that the significance of a native metaphysical belief lies not in its veracity in some absolute sense but in what it can tell us about a culture. "Is a mountain a sacred place? Does a river follow the ancestral path of an anaconda?" he asks, suggesting that answers to questions like these distort the meaning of native beliefs. "What matters," he says, "is the potency of the belief and the way the conviction plays out in the day to day life of people. A child raised to believe that a mountain is the abode of a protective spirit will be a profoundly different human being from a youth brought up to believe that a mountain is an inert mass of rock ready to be mined."[42] The symbolic enactment of winds among the natives of the Sibundoy Valley tells us about life experiences rooted in particular environments that function as responses to the quest for meaning.

NOTES

1. There are different denominations of yajé, both in native, in Spanish, and in other languages: yage, yaje, ayahuasca, ayaguasca. In this chapter, when I comment or refer to scholarly reports on yajé, I use the term that the scholar in question uses. When I refer to the practice and use within the Kamëntšá culture, I simple write "yajé."
2. Like in previous chapters, while I mention the two native groups of the Sibundoy Valley, I center my analysis on the scholarship and the stories of Kamëntša, my native community.
3. Bristol, in 1965, wrote, "No social classes have been observed among the Sibundoy, the only basis of personal interaction being strongly egalitarian. . . . A very few individuals (tatšumbua), both men and women, are recognized for their outstanding knowledge of medicinal and narcotic plants, for their familiarity with disease (Šokan), and for their ability to prepare remedies, either simple (Šěnan) or compound (Šěnan-jua-uam). Their services are paid for in cash, in kind, or in labor; their garden chores are often performed by recent patients." Melvin Lee Bristol, "Sibundoy Ethnobotany" (PhD diss., Harvard University, 1965), 24.
4. In 1969, Bristol wrote, "The preparation of *biaxíi* [yajé] is reserved to a small hut, *biaxíi wabwanái tambo* (biaxíi cooking shelter). . . . It is believed that should a pregnant woman come too near the hut, thunder and lightning will appear, and both the woman and the medicine-man will be killed instantly. Among other things, this taboo servers to prevent women's learning how to prepare *biaxíi* and thus intoxicate themselves when their husbands are travelling." Cfr. Melvin Lee Bristol, "The Psychotropic Banisteriopsis Among the Sibundoy of Colombia," *Botanical Museum Leaflets Harvard University* 21, no. 5 (March 1969): 126.
5. Haydeé Seijas, "The Medical System of the Sibundoy Indians of Colombia" (PhD diss., Tulane University, 1969), 38.
6. The presence of physicians has not been considered a threat to the native spirituality, in part because native and not-native physicians alike partake of yajé rituals and recognize its spiritual benefits.
7. It is also worth noting that dreaming of white technology, like cars, helicopters, radios, or TVs, suggests one should be prepared to speak with white people.
8. "Tcojotená bëts pato y tbjojtseftëtše, ana bejaye binyía jtsatsajanjam chka" [If one dreamed of a duck biting one, one will become sick next time one crosses a river]. "Buyeshiñe jtsetëjojuanama tcjojotjenase, ana betsko šokana joniynama" [If one dreams that one is drowning, one will soon become sick]. Justo Jacanamijoy España et al., *Camëntša Cabëngbe Ntšayanana* (Sibundoy: Uámana Soyënga Camëntšañe Uatsjéndayënga, 1994), 5.
9. Scholars who do not cite Chantre and Herrera, start with the story of the yajé as described by English Botanist Richard Spruce.
10. José Chantre y Herrera, "First Known Printed Reference to Ayahusca," in *Ayahuasca Reader: Encounters with the Amazon's Sacred Vine*, 2nd ed., ed. Luis Eduardo Luna and Steven F. White (Santa Fe: Synergetic Press, 2016), 142.
11. José Chantre y Herrera uses the Spanish word "adivino," a word to indicate more the capacity of a person to *see* the future. In the original Spanish, it is clear that Priest José Chantre, in describing yajé drink as *infernal brebaje*, means "devilish," "infernal." Ibid., 142–44.
12. My translation. The text in Spanish is as follows: "[El arte de la divinación] consiste simplemente en emborracharse, tener cara para mentir desvergonzadamente y hallar arte para descifrar á su modo los enigmas, lo cual no es ciertamente difícil entre aquellas gentes rudas y bozales." White and Luna translate the Spanish adjectives "rudas y bozales" as "simple and

stupid." In translating them as "barbarous and uncouth," I intend to carry the original meaning of *bozal* in Spanish. *Bozal* is literally "muzzle," and as an adjective, it was used to refer to black people who were taken as slaves and who could not speak Spanish well. In this context, it is important to remember that priests were not immune to the European prejudice that non-Europeans were largely less human than the Europeans.

13. Spruce is often cited as the "first" to have witnessed yajé ceremonies. For a more detailed historical report on yajé rituals, see: Bristol, "The Psychotropic Banisteriopsis," 113–18.

14. Richard Spruce, "On Some Remarkable Narcotics of the Amazon Valley and Orinoco," in *The Ayahuasca Reader*, 136–37.

15. Ibid.

16. Ibid., 141.

17. Ibid., 138.

18. It is worth noting that at present scholarship suggest that the Tukanos are the only group to have associated the yajé with a woman. All other native groups tell the story of the yajé in terms of a council of men. Cfr. Gerardo Reichel-Dolmatoff, "Yajé: Myth and Ritual," in *The Ayahuasca Reader*, 38–41.

19. Ibid.

20. This articulation of the yajé ceremony, as giving a power of vision and transformation, remains fundamental in the description of yajé experiences. In the *Birth of Tragedy*, Nietzsche wrote that a more fundamental reality comes alive when a festival breaks the *principium individuationis*. Yajé ceremonies also break this principle, but the process of intoxication, so to speak, remains in a more private and personal setting than in a public one.

21. Because I want to center the discussion of yajé as a ritual of healing as it is practiced in the lands of Sibundoy, I do not address the political complexities of the diversification of yajé rituals in urban areas. Part of the rituals of healing, I believe, presuppose a symbolic horizon of interpretation that loses part of its meaning in other cultural contexts. With this assertion, I do not intend to close off the possibility of having meaningful rituals of healing in cities, but I believe that the horizon of interpretation of the yajé ritual might change, depending on its context, purpose, and use. I am here limiting my discussion of yajé rituals within the Kamëntšá culture and within its symbolic understanding of the world. There are many reports of people partaking in yajé rituals in the Sibundoy Valley or in other areas of the Amazon with different purposes. See: Bristol, "The Psychotropic Banisteriopsis," 130–33. For a detailed description of the diaries of a "famous" yajé drinker, see: Jimmy Weiskopf, *Yaje: The New Purgatory* (Bogotá: Villegas Editores, 2004). Weiskopf has traveled through the Amazon basin, including the Putumayo region, understanding the yajé ritual in terms of a spiritual journey. He describes his revelations as pathways to divinity. While Weiskopf confesses himself atheist, he nonetheless describes his journeys as "purgatory," alluding more to the Christian soul that journeys from hell to paradise.

22. Alhena Caicedo Fernández indicates that the arrival of native doctors guiding yajé rituals to small groups of intellectuals, academics, and artists started in Colombian cities like Pasto, Bogota, Cali, Medellin, and Pereira in the 1990s. She also indicates that since then the ritual has started to gain adepts among university students. Cfr. Alhena Caicedo Fernández, "El Uso Ritual de Yajé: Patrimonialización y Consumo en Debate," *Revista Colombiana de Antropología* 46, no. 1 (Enero–Junio 2010): 66. In the paper here referred, Caicedo Fernández agrees that many medicine men had tried to deter "false" doctors from using the medicine inadequately.

23. See, for example, a report by Ariel Levy, a staff writer for the *New Yorker*, on the ayahuasca usage in some cities of the United States: https://www.newyorker.com/magazine/2016/09/12/the-ayahuasca-boom-in-the-u-s.

24. While at present there are no negative reports of people drinking yajé in Sibundoy, in other places of Latin America, there are tragic reports. Perhaps the most famous was reported in 2014, when a person died after taking yajé. For details on these news, see: https://www.cnn.com/2014/10/24/justice/ayahuasca-death-kyle-nolan-mother/index.html.

25. Bernd Brabec de Mori, "Tracing Hallucinations: Contributing to an Critical Ethnohistory of Ayahuasca Usage in the Peruvian Amazon," in *The Internationalization of Ayahuasca*, ed. Beatriz Caiuby Labate and Henrik Jungaberle (Berlin: Lit Verlag, 2011), 46.

26. Ibid., 27.

27. Ibid., 27.

28. Ibid., 26.

29. Ibid., 24.

30. Bristol, "Sibundoy Ethnobotany," 87.

31. Bristol, "The Psychotropic Banisteriopsis,"130–33. In regard to the description of yajé cooking, Lee Bristol wrote, "With the bark of B. caapi and the leaves of the next species, an hallucinogenic beverage is prepared in the following manner. (A medicine-man's instructions are given, though his practice was observed to be variously abbreviated.) Beginning in the morning, boil 40 litres of water, add a pile of bark scrapings (B. caapi) to the boiling water and stuff the pot full of leaves (B. rusbyana Mort.). At noon throw out both the shavings and the leaves and add the same amounts of fresh shavings and leaves, counting to boil for another three of four hours. Again, remove the shavings and leaves but this time add only '12 pairs of chagrupanga' (24 leaves of B. rusbyana), boiling them for two additional hours. When they are taken out, the pot is to cool and the beverage is then ready to take. (In practice, the quantities were variable and the boiling times shortened. Any beverage remaining from a previous preparation was added during the process.). . . . The preparation of Yagé is reserved to a small hut about 50 meters from the house. Women are expected to keep away from the area of the hut at all times. It is believed that should a pregnant woman approach the hut, thunder and lightning will appear, and both the woman and the medicine-man will be killed instantly." Bristol, "Sibundoy Ethnobotany," 207–10.

32. Evil winds, she says, is a concept analogous to the Hispano-American phenomenon of *susto* or magical fright. Cfr. Seijas, "The Medical System," 6.

33. Ibid, 135.

34. John Holmes McDowell, *Sayings of the Ancestors: The Spiritual Life of the Sibundoy Indians* (Lexington: University Press of Kentucky, 1989), vii.

35. In the literature on Native Americans, there are significant reports on the divine grounds for healing purposes. Closest to my grandfather's experience is Kiowa's story of the origin of their *Tai-me*. "Long ago there were bad times. The Kiowas were hungry and there was no food. There was a man who heard his children cry from hunger, and he went out to look for food. He walked four days and became very weak. On the fourth day he came to a great canyon. Suddenly there was thunder and lightning. A voice spoke to him and said, 'Why are you following me? What do you want?' The man was afraid. The thing standing before him had the feet of a deer, and its body was covered with feathers. The man answered that the Kiowas were hungry. 'Take me with you,' the voice said, 'and I will give you whatever you want.' From that day Tai-me has belonged to the Kiowas." Cf. N. Scott Momaday, *The Way to Rainy Mountain* (Albuquerque: University of New Mexico Press, 1969), 36. In the 1960s, while observing the rituals of healing, Seijas wrote, "The crystals . . . are small pieces of quartz that occasionally can be found in rivers, and although by chance anyone may find them, those owned by medicine man are said to be special in that the latter learn from yagé visions where to find them." Seijas, "The Medical System," 138.

36. In many respects, the story of my grandfather is like the experience related by Black Elk. As I do not intend to do comparative philosophy here, I only want to indicate the similarity of native religious experiences.

37. Similar experiences of preparation in a spiritual journey have been reported in other living indigenous groups. Perhaps the most well-known examples in North American come from Black Elk and from Carlos Castañeda's *The Teachings of Don Juan: A Yaqui Way of Knowledge*. Juan Matus, a Yaqui Indian Sorcerer, led Carlos Castaneda to the cognition of the shamans of ancient Mexico. Castañeda explains that for Don Juan it is imperative for human beings "to realize that the only thing that matters is their encounter with infinity." And that the way to do this is through seeing, not physically, but metaphysically, that is, the act of perceiving everything directly as it flows in the universe. Carlos Castañeda, *The Teachings of Don*

Juan: A Yaqui Way of Knowledge, 30th anniversary edition (New York: Washington Square Press, 1998), xvi.

38. Omar García Chivirí has indicated that when the Kamëntšá language is used for healing purposes, it becomes a "ritual language," by which he means that a fundamental part of the sacred healing is distorted if the language itself does not acquire a form of mystery. I believe Chivirri's interpretation is also true of the Inga language. Cfr. Omar Alberto García Chivirí. *Rezar, Cantar, Soplar: Etnografía de una Lengua Ritual* (Quito, Ecuador: Ediciones Ayba-Yala, 2004), 43–44.

39. *Baknašanayšá*, in Kamëntšá.

40. Seijas noted that "under the category of evil wind, the Sibundoy include all types of illnesses and symptoms believed to have resulted from certain types of experiences. Usually, but not exclusively, such experiences are in one way or another associated with death or the dead." Seijas, "The Medical System," 113.

41. Hugo Jamioy, *Bínÿbe Oboyejuayëng: Danzantes del Viento : Poesía Bilingüe* (Bogotá: Ministerio de Cultura, 2010), 62. *Uábeman* means writing, but in the context Jamioy is using it, it signifies also "expression from the heart."

42. Wade Davis, *Light at the Edge of the World : A Journey through the Realm of Vanishing Cultures* (Vancouver: Douglas and McIntyre, 2007), 65.

Conclusion

In Sibundoy Putumayo, at the basin of the Andean Mountains in the southwest of Colombia where a beautiful valley fuses the Andean highlands with the Amazonian basin, the Kamëntšá and Inga peoples keep their symbolic representations and their concerns about life and existence alive as efforts to answer to the quest for meaning, even in the face of the colonial undertaking and despite imposed efforts of cultural assimilation. Taking the idea of radical empiricism exposed by William James in *The Meaning of Truth* as a methodological tool to understanding the symbolism of native cultures, in the previous chapters I discussed the constituted and constituting nature of the symbols of the Kamëntšá culture: Time as history and storytelling, Beauty as dancing, the Spirit as enacted in rituals of healing.

I argued that the nature of those native symbols lies in its dual nature. On the one hand, they are constituted symbols; they function as forces of the past that constrain the interpretative horizon of value-formation of the present and the future but do not determine the quest for meaning entirely. Kamëntšá symbols depend on oral tradition and rituals that are historically rooted in Tabanok, the sacred place of origins for the Kamëntšá culture and language. But the Kamëntšá symbols also constitute life and meaning. They enact a form of understanding existence and are subject to creative interpretation. They reflect the present character of the community and are suggestive condensations of the feelings of its members.

The vitality of symbols came upon reflecting on the nature of living cultural experiences. I argued that the enactment of stories, of dancing, and of rituals of healing in the Kamëntšá culture suggests that symbols remain grounded in life experiences, providing them with meaning and value. These symbols are also alive in the sense that they are not mere representations of human thought but creative answers, enactments of the quest for meaning.

Because of this dual symbolic nature present in the Kamëntšá culture, one should not take the value of native symbolism merely on its antiquity. To be sure, the antiquity of oral tradition teaches us about sensibilities that humans develop in those settings, like the ability to interpret the environment as a home. Central to the Kamëntšá culture is that we see the Sibundoy Valley as a place that must be taken care of; that care extends to the other people who live in the valley, however different they look, ultimately as members of the same place of origin that must be cared for and valued.

In the introduction, in addition to a brief explanation of "symbols" and "experience," I appropriated the idea of radical empiricism as James articulated in this work *The Meaning of Truth* and I applied it to my own cultural context. I also used the concept of fulfillment and completion that John Dewey discusses in *Art as Experience*, and I incorporated it into the discussion on the nature of Kamëntšá symbols. Implicit in my taking these ideas is a critique of the view that symbols are a detached representation of experience, as the followers of the Enlightenment have articulated, especially Ernst Cassirer and Eliade. More explicitly, I expressed my disagreement with the interpretative work presented by John McDowell, who assumed that the narrative experiences among Kamëntšás are remnants of an old mythology.

In chapter 1, I discussed time. I started with a discussion of Kamëntšá notions of their place of origin and their idea of nature as symbolic and material. I presented a scholarly history of the Sibundoy Valley since the times of the Spanish Conquest in 1535 to the most devastating form of colonization in the last century. I concluded indicating that historical evidence suggests that the lands of the native groups of the Sibundoy Valley dwindled significantly with the arrival of the Spaniards to the region, especially in the first half of the last century, affecting the language, the culture, and the perception of the native communities. The purpose of including this historical account was to account for the material conditions from which symbols of the Sibundoy Valley have emerged. Because I take life experience as the ground of my study, I wanted to account for the sociohistorical circumstances that have shaped the living symbols of the native cultures of the valley. Next, I discussed time as storytelling. The main argument was that the content is a necessary but insufficient condition to account for the meaning of a native story. The tone and force in the act of telling a story are as significant as the content of the story. Experientially, it is not the same to ask natives for a story to further scholarship and to ask them for the meaning of life, of the good, of cultural change, and receive a story as an answer. When one is immersed deeply in a cultural environment, one notices that a horizon of interpretation changes before the act of telling stories. In including reflective accounts of North American storytellers, I held that my analysis of the experience of storytelling came from my experience but was not limited to it.

In the second chapter, I discussed the Bětskanté as a constituted and constituting symbol of Beauty. I argued that the foundational stories of Bětskanté function as powerful past forces that charge the annual dancing with value. But I claimed that the most significant part of the dancing does not come from the foundation of the stories, but from the enactment of Beauty. I argued that behind all its cultural transformations, the Bětskanté is a celebration of life and existence as it fundamentally comes, with all its tragedy and hope, with its actuality and possibility. In describing the process of reconnection through dancing and forgiveness, I indicated that the dancing is a genuine aesthetic experience, an act of reunification with all the families and with the fundamental forces of life. I took the Bětskanté to be a celebration of a philosophy of life.

Finally, in the third chapter, I argued that the rituals of healing, especially the yajé ritual, suggest a metaphysical view of Sibundoy. I argued that the rituals of healing presuppose an ontology of winds, a notion that winds are both physical and metaphysical forces that may exert power over the health of individuals. I indicated that the nature of ritual language in healing ceremonies naturally accounts for constituted meanings of the rituals. In describing the nature of the medicine men who practice yajé ceremonies and the experiences of healing, I suggest that behind all the rituals of healing, there is a metaphysical understanding of human life. One can learn that the ontology of the winds is reflective of the capacity of humans to charge their natural relations with their environments with symbolic meaning that has the power to heal or to cause harm.

I reached the above conclusions on reading interpretative works of the Kaměntšá culture and on thinking about my own life experience. I noticed that most of the approaches to the native cultures are fragmentary, taking one or another aspect of the culture but without providing a solid foundation. I think the works of previous scholars, like the writings of Bristol, Seijas, Juajibioy, and McDowell, have led me to take the symbolic structure of the Kaměntšá culture to philosophical interpretation. Likewise, I think that my experience as a member of the community, born and raised in this place, facilitated my analysis. The philosophical engagement with my life, with the activity of self-questioning with the purpose of finding meaning, came to me slowly, in a significant part out of the time and dedication of my philosophy professors with my education, both in the United States and in Colombia. I hope that this interpretive work fosters a more productive discussion on the nature of symbolic meaning in specific cultural contexts. I believe that an understanding of other cultures requires a comprehension of what other people believe and why they believe what they believe.

Bibliography

Alexander, Hartley Burr. *The World's Rim: Great Mysteries of the North American Indians.* Lincoln: University of Nebraska Press, 1953.
Alexander, Thomas M. *The Human Eros: Eco-Ontology and the Aesthetics of Existence.* New York: Fordham University Press, 2013.
Bahamón, Misael Kuan S. J. "La Misión Capuchina en el Caquetá y el Putumayo 1893–1929." Master's thesis, Pontifica Universidad Javeriana Bogotá, 2013.
Barrera Jurado, Gloria Stella. *Autonomía Artesanal: Creaciones y Resistencias del Pueblo Kamsá.* Bogotá: Pontificia Universidad Javeriana, 2015.
Bonilla, Víctor Daniel. *Siervos de Dios y Amos de Indios: El Estado y la Misión Capuchina en el Amazonas.* Bogotá: Stella, 1969.
Brabec de Mori, Bernd. "Tracing Hallucinations: Contributing to an Critical Ethnohistory of Ayahuasca Usage in the Peruvian Amazon." In *The Internationalization of Ayahuasca*, edited by Beatriz Caiuby Labate and Henrik Jungaberle, 23–48. Berlin: Lit Verlag, 2011.
Bristol, Melvin Lee. "The Psychotropic Banisteriopsis Among the Sibundoy of Colombia." *Botanical Museum Leaflets Harvard University* 21, no. 5 (March 1969): 113–40.
———. "Sibundoy Ethnobotany." PhD diss., Harvard University, 1965.
Caicedo Fernández, Alhena. "El Uso Ritual de Yajé: Patrimonialización y Consumo en Debate." *Revista Colombiana de Antropología* 46, no. 1 (Enero–Junio 2010): 63–86.
Cassirer, Ernst. *An Essay on Man.* New Haven, CT: Yale University Press, 1967.
———. *Mythical Thought*, vol. 2 of *The Philosophy of the Symbolic Forms.* New Haven, CT: Yale University Press, 1955.
Castañeda, Carlos. *The Teachings of Don Juan: A Yaqui Way of Knowledge*, 30th anniversary edition. New York: Washington Square Press, 1998.
Chantre y Herrera, José. "First Known Printed Reference to Ayahusca." In *Ayahuasca Reader: Encounters with the Amazon's Sacred Vine*, 2nd ed, edited by Luis Eduardo Luna and Steven F. White, 142–44. Santa Fe: Synergetic Press, 2016.
Congreso de la República de Colombia. "Ley Número 35 de 27-02-1888." *Diario Oficial No. 7311* (1888).
Davis, Wade. *Light at the Edge of the World: A Journey through the Realm of Vanishing Cultures.* Vancouver: Douglas and McIntyre, 2007.
De Castellví, Marcelino. "Historia Eclesiástica de la Amazonía Colombiana." *Revista Universidad Pontificia Bolivariana* 10, no. 36 (1944): 483–596.
De Castellví, Marcelino, and Lucas Espinosa. *Propedeútica Etnioglotológica y Diccionario Classificador de las Lenguas Indoamericanas.* Madrid: Consejo Superior de Investigaciones Científicas, 1958.

De Friedemann, Nina S. "Niveles Contemporáneos de Indigenismo en Colombia: Aculturación, Deculturación, etnocidio e indigenismo." In *Indigenismo y Aniquilamiento de Indígenas en Colombia*, edited by Juan Friede, Nina S. de Friedemann, and Dario Fajardo. Bogotá: Universidad Nacional de Colombia, 1975.

De Plaza, Jose Antonio. *Memorias para la Historia de la Nueva Granada*. Bogotá: Imprenta del Neogranadino, 1850.

De Quito, Jacinto Ma. *Historia de la Fundación del Pueblo de San Francisco en el Valle de Sibundoy*. Sibundoy: Edición Cicela, 1952.

Dewey, John. *Art as Experience*. New York: Penguin Group, 1934.

Diagnostico Plan Salvaguarda. *Sboachan Jtabouashëntsam Natjëmban Nÿestkang Jtsyëñëngam: Sembrando el Maiz, Fruto de la Fuerza y la Esperanza para asegurar el Buen Vivir Camëntšá*. Sibundoy: Cabildo Indígena Camëntšá, Ministerio del Interior, 2012.

Documento Communidad Camëntšá. *Procesos de Tranformación y Alternativas de Autgestión Indígena*. Bogotá: Editorial ABC, 1989.

Eliade, Mircea. *Myth and Reality*. Translated by Willard R. Trask. Long Grove, IL: Harper & Row, 1963.

———. *Myth of the Eternal Return*. Translated by Willard R. Trask. Princeton, NJ: Princeton University Press, 1954.

Escobedo, Tricia. "Teen's Quest for Amazon 'Medicine' Ends in Tragedy." CNN. October 27, 2014.https://www.cnn.com/2014/10/24/justice/ayahuasca-death-kyle-nolan-mother/index.html.

Friede, Juan. "Archivo General de Indias—Sevilla. Patronato, legajo 189. Ramo 35." *Anuario Colombiano de Historia Social y de la Cultura* 4 (1969): 123–30.

———. *El Indio en Lucha por la Tierra: Historia de los Resguardos del Macizo Central Colombiano*. Bogotá: Ediciones La Chispa, 1944.

———. "Leyendas de Nuestro Señor de Sibundoy y el Santo Carlos Tamabioy." *Boletín de Arqueología* 1, no. 4 (Julio–Agosto 1945): 315–19.

Garzón Chivirí, Omar Alberto. *Rezar, Cantar, Soplar: Etnografía de una Lengua Ritual*. Quito, Ecuador: Ediciones Ayba-Yala, 2004.

Jacanamijoy España, Justo, Juan Bautista Jacanamijoy Juajibioy, and Carlos Jamioy Narváez. *Camëntša Cabëngbe Ntšayanana*. Sibundoy: Uámana Soyënga Camëntšañe Uatsjéndayënga, 1994.

James, William. *Essays in Radical Empiricism*. Cambridge, MA: Harvard University Press, 1976.

———. "On Some Omissions of Introspective Psychology." *Mind* 9, no. 33 (January 1884): 1–26.

———. *Writings 1902–1910*. New York: The Library of America, 1987.

Jamioy, Hugo. *Bínÿbe Oboyejuayëng: Danzantes del Viento : Poesía Bilingüe*. Bogotá: Ministerio de Cultura, 2010.

Juajibioy, Alberto. *Lenguaje Ceremonial y Narraciones Tradicionales de la Cultura Kamëntšá*. México City: Fondo de Cultura Económica, 2008.

Juajibioy, Alberto, and Alvaro Wheeler. *Bosquejo Etnolingüístico del Grupo Kamsá de Sibundoy Putumayo, Colombia*. Bogotá: Instituto Lingüístico de Verano, 1973.

King, Thomas. *The Truth about Stories: A Native Narrative*, 1st ed. Minneapolis: University of Minnesota Press, 2008.

Krasten, Rafael. *The Civilization of the South American Indians: With a Special Reference to Magic and Religion*. New York: Knopf, 1926.

Levinsohn, Stephen H. *The Inga Language*. The Hague, Netherlands: Mouton & Co. B.V. Publishers, 1976.

Levy, Ariel. "The Drug of Choice for the Age of Kale." *New Yorker*. September 12, 2016.https://www.newyorker.com/magazine/2016/09/12/the-ayahuasca-boom-in-the-u-s.

McDonald, Margaret Read, ed. *Traditional Storytelling Today: An International Sourcebook*. New York: Routledge, 1999.

McDowell, John Holmes. "Exemplary Ancestors and Pernicious Spirits: Sibundoy Concepts of Cultural Evolution." In *Traditional Storytelling Today: An International Sourcebook*, edited by Margaret Read MacDonald. Chicago: Fitzroy Dearborn Publishers, 1999.

———. *Sayings of the Ancestors: The Spiritual Life of the Sibundoy Indians*. Lexington: University Press of Kentucky, 1989.
———. *So Wise Were Our Elders*. Lexington: University Press of Kentucky, 1994.
Momaday, N. Scott. *The Man Made of Words*. New York: St Martin's Griffin, 1997.
———. *The Way to Rainy Mountain*. Albuquerque: University of New Mexico Press, 1969.
Nietzsche, Friedrich. *The Birth of Tragedy*. Translated by Walter Kaufmann. New York: Vintage Books, 1967.
Princeton Theological Seminary Library. "Las Misiones en Colombia: Obra de los Misioneros Capuchinos, de la Delegación Apostólica, del Gobierno y de la Junta Arquidiocesana Nacional en el Caquetá y Putumayo." Princeton Theological Seminary Library.https://archive.org/details/lasmisionesencol00unse(accessed July 2017).
Read, Margaret M. (Ed). *Traditional Storytelling Today: An International Sourcebook*. New York: Routledge, 1999.
Reichel-Dolmatoff, Gerardo, "Yajé: Myth and Ritual," in *The Ayahuasca Reader: Encounters with the Amazon's Sacred Vine*, 2nd ed., edited by Luis Eduardo Luna and Steven F. White, 38–41. Santa Fe: Synergetic Press, 2016.
Richard Evan. "A New Narcotic Genus from the Amazon Slope of the Colombian Andes." *Botanical Museum Leaflets, Harvard University* 17, no. 1 (1955): 1–11.
Seijas, Haydeé. "The Medical System of the Sibundoy Indians of Colombia." PhD diss., Tulane University, 1969.
Spruce, Richard. "On Some Remarkable Narcotics of the Amazon Valley and Orinoco." In *The Ayahuasca Reader: Encounters with the Amazon's Sacred Vine*, 2nd ed., edited by Luis Eduardo Luna and Steven F. White, 136–41. Santa Fe: Synergetic Press, 2016.
Tambiah, Stanley Jeyaraja. *Magic, Science, Religion, and the Scope of Rationality*. Cambridge: Cambridge University Press, 1990.
Tandioy Jansasoy, Francisco, and Stephen H. Levinsohn. *Diccionario Inga*. Santiago, Putumayo: Comité de Educación Inga de la Organización Musu Runakuna, 1997.
Taussig, Michael. *Shamanism, Colonialism, and the Wild Man: A Study in Terror and Healing*. Chicago: University of Chicago Press, 1987.
Triana, Miguel. *Por el Sur de Colombia: Excursion Pintoresca y Científica al Putumayo*. Bogotá: Biblioteca Popular de Cultura Colombiana, 1907.
Uribe, Simón. *Frontier Road: Power, History, and the Everyday State in the Colombian Amazon*. West Sussex, UK: John Wiley & Sons, 2017.
Vidal, Ramón. "Critica histórica al libro de Victor D. Bonilla, 'Siervos de Dios y Amos de Indios.'" *Separata de Cultura Nariñense*, no. 25 (Julio 1970).
Weiskopf, Jimmy. *Yaje: The New Purgatory*. Bogotá: Villegas Editores, 2004.

Index

Alexander, Thomas M., 29
Ayahuasca, 69; Preparation of, 86n31. *See also* Yajé

Banisteria caapi, 67. *See also* Ayahuasca
Beauty, 30, 49; aesthetics and, 32, 58, 81; experiences of the, 47, 61n19; languages and, 36; meaning of, 58–59
Bětšknaté, 45; constituting symbol, 52; constituted symbol, 47; dancing, 53; meaning of, 47. *See also* culture, Inga
Bonilla, Victor D., 9

Cassirer, E., 31, 42n97, 57
Clestrinÿë, 51
Colonialization, 3, 4; cultural ruptures from, 16; economic institutions of, 4; land conquest, 3; legal justifications of, 8, 12; narratives of, 15, 23; slavery, 11; Spanish Conquest, 3, 5; spiritual conquest, 5, 6; struggles against, 6, 81; territory and, 11–14

Dewey, J., 28, 29, 58

Eliade, M., 27, 31

Inga natives, 2; culture, 45; dreams, 22, 24, 50; language, 22, 24, 42n88, 60n18; land, 3, 6; stories, 21

James, W., 28, 89

Kamëntšá natives, 2; dreams, 24; language as experience, 2; metaphysics of, 51, 63; rituals of forgiveness, 55; rituals of healing, 64; rituals of transformation, 82; catholic influence, 52, 55, 56; sociolinguistics, 54
King, T., 31

Lee, Bristol M., 3; Sibundoy ethnobotany, 70, 85n21

Malinowski, B., 71
Momaday, N. Scott, 29
Mother Earth, 2, 46, 48, 60n5; Religious symbol of, 55; Cultural meaning of, 59; Nature as, 51, 81; Inga's view of, 2
McDowell, J., 19, 21, 28, 49; Critical views, 72

Nietzsche, Fredrich, 57

Philosophy of culture, 29, 42n97; dancing as, 57; life as, 47, 56, 57; metaphysics as, 66

Reichel-Dolmatoff, G., 68

Sacredness, 2; Drinks, 77; Stories, 2, 18, 27; Language of the, 20, 31; Heart, 54;

Instruments, 78; Places of the, 3, 4, 16, 53, 55, 83
Seijas, H., 71
Schultes, Richard E., 70
Sibundoy Valley, 2, 5; History of the, 4, 5, 40n54; Cultural meaning of, 2; Land Division of, 8; Catholic missionaries, 5, 8–9, 56
Spirit, 22, 24; Conceptions of the, 24, 26; Culture as, 29; Dancing, 52, 55; Metaphysics of, 66, 78; Narratives of the, 35, 72; Voices of the, 31; Wilderness, 48. *See also* Wind
Spruce, R., 67
Storytelling, 18, 20; Experience of, 18, 19; Difference between myth and, 18; Constituting meaning, 28. *See also* Time

Tamabioy Carlos, 2, 3, 6, 38n7, 40n54; Native leadership, 6
Time, 3; Constituted symbol, 19, 20; Constituting symbol, 19, 28, 32; Anthropological accounts, 24, 25; History as, 1, 2, 3, 16; Sacredness of, 27; Storytelling as, 2, 18, 19, 29; Primary experience, 2, 17, 30

Wade, D., 83
Wind, 51; Language of, 81; Ontology of, 80, 82, 83; Metaphysics of, 81; Personification of, 71; Poetics of the, 81

Yajé, 66; Ethnobotany, 66; Experiences of, 73; Ceremony of, 73; Constituting symbol, 73; Personal accounts, 66–79; Woman, 68

www.ingramcontent.com/pod-product-compliance
Lightning Source LLC
Chambersburg PA
CBHW021852300426
44115CB00005B/136